Financial Performance

Financial Performance

Marc Bertoneche and Rory Knight

OXFORD AUCKLAND BOSTON JOHANNESBURG MELBOURNE NEW DELHI

Butterworth-Heinemann
Linacre House, Jordan Hill, Oxford OX2 8DP
225 Wildwood Avenue, Woburn, MA 01801-2041
A division of Reed Educational and Professional Publishing Ltd

   A member of the Reed Elsevier plc group

First published 2001

British Library Cataloguing in Publication Data
Bertoneche, Marc
   Financial performance
   1. Corporations – Finance – Management
   I. Title   II. Knight, Rory
   658.1′5

ISBN 0 7506 4011 1

Composition by Genesis Typesetting, Laser Quay, Rochester, Kent
Printed and bound in Great Britain

FOR EVERY TITLE THAT WE PUBLISH, BUTTERWORTH-HEINEMANN
WILL PAY FOR BTCV TO PLANT AND CARE FOR A TREE.

Contents

Introduction   vii

Part 1   Performance Measurement

1   Review of financial statements 1: The balance sheet   3

2   Review of financial statements 2: The income statement
    and the statement of cash flows   46

3   Assessing financial health   74

Part 2   Valuation

4   The cost of capital: concept and measurement   109

5   Valuation: principles and methods   137

6   Shareholder value: A European perspective   164

Index   203

Introduction

This book presents the foundation concepts underlying the Senior Executive Programmes we have taught together and separately over the last fifteen years in Europe, Asia and North America.

We have learned a great deal from the thousands of senior executives with whom we have had the privilege to work.

These programmes include

The Oxford Advanced Management Programme
The Oxford Senior Executive Finance Programme
The INSEAD Advanced Management Programme
The IMI, Geneva, Advanced Management Programme
The Harvard Advanced Management Programme
The Oxford International Executive Programme, Singapore
The IMI International Finance Programme, Singapore

The book is intended as a reference manual as well as a text book and will be of value to anyone with an interest in financial performance – particularly senior executives.

The developments in modern finance over the last two decades have implications for the way that senior executives think about the finance discipline. It is no longer enough to have a rudimentary knowledge of basic finance and a heavy reliance on financial specialists

CEOs of course need excellent financial professionals – however, they need to go beyond this and provide strategic leadership. This requires a conceptual framework for dealing with financial matters.

Our teaching programmes aim to provide this framework and this book provides a description of the underlying ideas.

Figure I.1 illustrates the architecture of the book. The book revolves around the concept of value and it is organized into two parts.

Part 1 Performance Measurement

This part consists of three chapters, all of which focus on the real and fairly complex set of financial statements of DaimlerChrysler AG.

The first two chapters provide a detailed guided tour of the financial statements which deconstructs the complexity and then reconstructs the financials to provide a clearer base for analysis.

These chapters have been arranged to deal with each line item of the financial statements which have been highlighted in such a way as to allow the reader to treat the material as a reference as well as a sequential read.

In our experience the use of real financials is essential for a realistic foundation in the subject.

Chapter 3 presents a framework for evaluating financial health and introduces a cash flow based model for understanding the short and medium term constraints on a firm's growth. This exposition revolves around the concept of sustainable growth.

Part 2 Valuation

The second part of the book, like the first, consists of three chapters. Chapter 4 introduces the cost-of-capital concept and Chapter 5 provides a general source of reference for valuation and a variety of different applications.

Chapter 6 concludes the book with a review of the concept of shareholder value from a European perspective.

We thank Caroline Lomas and Denise Legge for their support in preparing the text. Our publisher, Mike Cash, deserves special thanks for his continued support and patience.

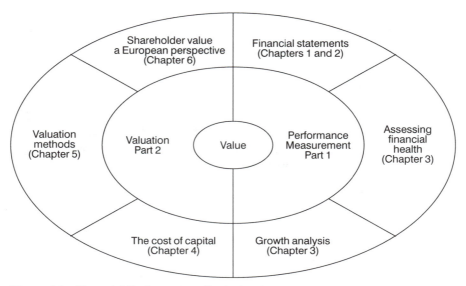

Figure I.1   Financial Performance: Book structure

Part 1

Performance Measurement

Review of financial statements 1: The balance sheet

1.1 Introduction

The financial statements of a firm represent the usual starting point for any assessment of financial performance. In particular, a valuation of a firm begins with a review of its current financial position and its recent results.

The review of financial statements is organized as two chapters which will focus in some detail on the financial statements of DaimlerChrysler AG, the international auto manufacturer, created by the fusion of the German Daimler and the US Chrysler corporations.

Our experience in working with senior executives over the years suggests that there is a benefit to starting the discussion of financial performance with an actual set of financial statements, despite some of the noise that this brings with it.

We chose DaimlerChrysler for a number of reasons. First, it comes from the largest industrial merger in history and therefore it is of itself an interesting company with which to become familiar. Second, it is the first company to report in Euros (€) and also in US$.* We felt that this feature would be helpful for the potential audience of this book. Third, it accounted for the merger using a 'pooling of interests' method rather than as a purchase. This means that the two companies are simply combined and so the new entity reflects the characteristics of the two companies on an integrated basis. Therefore the historic trends reported are more meaningful. The pooling method also avoids the accounting complications due to goodwill. Finally, the European orientation of this book dictated that we select a multinational in the European tradition. DaimlerChrysler now

---

* Note that throughout the text figures are in millions.

presents financial statements on a more transparent basis than most mainland European firms.

The Rhenish style of reporting is still, however, quite different from the Anglo American style and DaimlerChrysler does not conform entirely to the standard formats of display and disclosure that is usual for Anglo American firms.

The main objectives of this section of the book are:

1 To introduce the language and terminology of finance using a real set of financial statements.
2 To provide a method of re-arranging a set of financials to a format that is most conducive for assessing financial health and carrying out a valuation.
3 To provide a conceptual framework of the relationship among the three elements that constitute a set of financial statements (namely the balance sheet, the cash flow statement and the income statement) as a basis for valuation.
4 To develop a clear view of the flow of cash through a firm.

In short we aim to equip you with the ability to cut through a complex set of financial statements, to distil them down to their essence, and to form an insight into what value-critical information they contain.

The balance of the section is organized around the three key elements of financial statements, the balance sheet, the income statement and the cash flow statement which are reproduced as Exhibits 1.1 to 1.3 respectively exactly as reported by the company. The balance sheet is reviewed in this chapter and the other two statements in Chapter 2.

1.2 Deconstructing the balance sheet

Turning to the DaimlerChrysler balance sheet reproduced as Exhibit 1.4 one is confronted with not one but five different balance sheets.

Working from left to right the first untitled column we encounter is a description of the various line items in the balance sheet starting with Assets and working down to Total liabilities and stockholders' equity. The next column is headed 'Note' which refers to the notes to the financial statements. As mentioned in italics at the end of the page in Exhibit 1.1 the notes provide further information on the line item in question and they do form an integral part of the consolidated statements.

The next two columns reflect the consolidated balance sheets at 31 December 1998, first in dollars ($) (column 3) and then in Euros (€) (column 4). The consolidated balance sheet for 1997 in Euros (€) is

Exhibit 1.1 DaimlerChrysler balance sheet

CONSOLIDATED BALANCE SHEETS

(in millions)	Note	1998 (Note 1) $	1998 €	Consolidated At December 31, 1997 €	Financial Services At December 31, 1998 €	1997 €
Assets						
Intangible assets	10	3,004	2,561	2,422	104	51
Property, plant and equipment, net	10	34,649	29,532	28,558	53	39
Investments and long-term financial assets	16	3,344	2,851	2,397	632	631
Equipment on operating leases, net	11	17,203	14,662	11,092	12,001	9,571
Fixed assets		58,200	49,606	44,469	12,790	10,292
Inventories	12	13,840	11,796	10,897	654	505
Trade receivables	13	8,922	7,605	7,265	654	761
Receivables from financial services	14	31,054	26,468	21,717	26,460	21,658
Other receivables	15	12,642	10,775	11,376[1]	5,936	6,214
Securities	16	14,267	12,160	10,180	597	418
Cash and cash equivalents	17	7,731	6,589	6,809	681	702
Current assets		88,456	75,393	68,244	34,982	30,258
Deferred taxes	8	5,885	5,016	5,688	17	14
Prepaid expenses	19	7,197	6,134	6,430	133	71
Total assets (thereof short-term 1998: € 57,953; 1997: € 54,370)		159,738	136,149	124,831	47,922	40,635
Liabilities and stockholders' equity						
Capital stock		3,005	2,561	2,391		
Additional paid-in capital		8,534	7,274	2,958		
Retained earnings		24,091	20,533	21,892[1]		
Accumulated other comprehensive income		(1)	(1)	1,143		
Treasury stock		–	–	(424)		
Preferred stock		–	–			
Stockholders' equity	20	35,629	30,367	27,960	4,639	4,379
Minority interests		810	691	782	17	28
Accrued liabilities	22	40,629	34,629	35,787	412	508
Financial liabilities	23	47,436	40,430	34,375	36,810	31,381
Trade liabilities	24	15,074	12,848	12,026	242	90
Other liabilities	25	10,851	9,249	7,912	2,366	1,610
Liabilities		73,361	62,527	54,313	39,418	33,081
Deferred taxes	8	4,886	4,165	2,502	2,665	2,366
Deferred income	26	4,423	3,770	3,487	771	273
Total liabilities (thereof short-term 1998: € 58,181; 1997: € 50,918)		124,109	105,782	96,871	43,283	36,256
Total liabilities and stockholders' equity		159,738	136,149	124,831	47,922	40,635

[1] Includes a tax receivable/tax benefit of approximately € 1.49 billion relating to the special distribution (see Note 20).

The accompanying notes are an integral part of these Consolidated Financial Statements.
All balances have been restated from Deutsche Marks into Euros using the exchange rate as of January 1, 1999.

(Annual Report 1998, p. 69)

Exhibit 1.2 DaimlerChrysler income statement

CONSOLIDATED STATEMENTS OF INCOME

(in millions, except per share amounts)	Note	1998 (Note 1) $	Consolidated Year ended December 31, 1998 €	1997 €	1996 €	Financial Services Year ended December 31, 1998 €	1997 €	1996 €
Revenues	30	154,615	131,782	117,572	101,415	7,908	6,545	5,548
Cost of sales	5	(121,692)	(103,721)	(92,953)	(78,995)	(6,157)	(5,075)	(4,347)
Gross margin		32,923	28,061	24,619	22,420	1,751	1,470	1,201
Selling, administrative and other expenses	5	(19,041)	(16,229)	(15,621)	(13,902)	(921)	(760)	(652)
Research and development		(5,833)	(4,971)	(4,408)	(4,081)	–	–	–
Other income	6	1,425	1,215	957	848	106	82	58
Merger costs	1	(803)	(685)	–	–	–	–	–
Income before financial income and income taxes		8,671	7,391	5,547	5,285	936	792	607
Financial income, net	7	896	763	633	408	23	4	–
Income before income taxes and extraordinary item		9,567	8,154	6,180	5,693	959	796	607
Tax benefit relating to a special distribution				1,487[1]				
Income taxes				(1,005)[1]				
Total income taxes	8	(3,607)	(3,075)	482	(1,547)	(361)	(307)	(234)
Minority interest		(153)	(130)	(115)	23	(2)	(1)	(2)
Income before extraordinary item		5,807	4,949	6,547	4,169	596	488	371
Extraordinary item: loss on early extinguishment of debt, net of taxes	9	(151)	(129)	–	(147)	–	–	–
Net income		5,656	4,820	6,547[2]	4,022	596	488	371
Earnings per share	31							
Basic earnings per share								
Income before extraordinary item		6.05	5.16	6.90	4.24	–	–	–
Extraordinary item		(0.16)	(0.13)	–	(0.15)	–	–	–
Net income		5.89	5.03	6.90[2]	4.09	–	–	–
Diluted earnings per share								
Income before extraordinary item		5.91	5.04	6.78	4.20	–	–	–
Extraordinary item		(0.16)	(0.13)	–	(0.15)	–	–	–
Net income		5.75	4.91	6.78[3]	4.05	–	–	–

[1] Reflects the tax benefit relating to a special distribution (see Note 20).
[2] Includes non-recurring tax benefits of € 1,003 relating to the decrease in valuation allowance as of December 31, 1997, applied to the domestic operations that file a combined tax return.
[3] Excluding non-recurring tax benefits, 1997 net income would have been € 4,057 and basic and diluted earnings per share would have been € 4.28 and € 4.21, respectively.

The accompanying notes are an integral part of these Consolidated Financial Statements.
All balances have been restated from Deutsche Marks into Euros using the exchange rate as of January 1, 1999.

(Annual Report 1998 p. 68)

Exhibit 1.3 DaimlerChrysler cash flow statement

CONSOLIDATED STATEMENTS OF CASH FLOWS

(in millions)	1998 (Note 1) $	1998 €	1997 €	1996 €	1998 €	1997 €	1996 €
		Consolidated Year ended December 31,			Financial Services Year ended December 31,		
Net income	5,656	4,820	6,547	4,022	596	488	371
Income (loss) applicable to minority interests	153	130	115	(22)	2	1	2
Adjustments to reconcile net income to net cash provided by operating activities:							
Tax benefit relating to a special distribution	–	–	(1,487)	–	–	–	–
Gain on disposals of businesses	(347)	(296)	(569)	(182)	–	–	7
Depreciation and amortization of equipment on operating leases	2,314	1,972	1,456	1,159	1,784	1,429	1,215
Depreciation and amortization of fixed assets	6,287	5,359	4,847	4,233	38	27	23
Change in deferred taxes	2,298	1,959	(706)	112	399	288	83
Extraordinary item: loss on early extinguishment of debt	151	129	–	147	–	–	–
Change in financial instruments	(224)	(191)	146	200	–	–	2
(Gain) loss on disposal of fixed assets/securities	(432)	(368)	(204)	(65)	(51)	13	–
Change in trading securities	294	251	(387)	(171)	–	–	–
Change in accrued liabilities	1,665	1,419	840	1,416	44	3	21
Change in current assets and liabilities:							
– inventories, net	(1,145)	(976)	(744)	(427)	64	(140)	(49)
– trade receivables	(807)	(688)	(555)	53	124	23	4
– trade liabilities	2,144	1,827	1,709	231	159	1	(30)
– other assets and liabilities	1,564	1,334	1,329	(750)	1,107	1,187	(369)
Cash provided by operating activities	19,571	16,681	12,337	9,956	4,266	3,320	1,280
Purchases of fixed assets:							
– Increase in equipment on operating leases	(9,733)	(8,296)	(5,914)	(4,045)	(7,238)	(4,889)	(3,458)
– Purchases of property, plant and equipment	(9,568)	(8,155)	(8,051)	(6,721)	(37)	(24)	(12)
– Purchases of other fixed assets	(358)	(305)	(264)	(215)	(60)	(38)	(13)
Proceeds from disposals of equipment on operating leases	3,466	2,954	2,632	1,730	2,270	1,905	1,794
Proceeds from disposals of fixed assets	604	515	576	660	15	21	6
Payments for acquisitions of businesses	(1,006)	(857)	(607)	(236)	(43)	(64)	(83)
Proceeds from disposals of businesses	804	685	1,336	1,105	3	–	283
Additions to receivables from financial services	(95,264)	(81,196)	(70,154)	(56,880)	(81,259)	(71,221)	(58,126)
Repayments of receivables from financial services:							
– Finance receivables collected	39,638	33,784	22,257	15,892	33,784	23,114	17,042
– Proceeds from sales of finance receivables	48,046	40,950	44,336	39,474	40,950	44,336	39,474
Acquisitions of securities (other than trading)	(5,418)	(4,617)	(5,190)	(4,024)	(2,602)	(1,701)	(1,475)
Proceeds from sales of securities (other than trading)	3,208	2,734	3,828	4,649	2,487	1,763	2,382
Change in other cash	(1,926)	(1,641)	685	(134)	(187)	(739)	(656)
Cash used for investing activities	(27,507)	(23,445)	(14,530)	(8,745)	(11,917)	(7,537)	(2,842)
Change in commercial paper borrowings and short-term financial liabilities	2,937	2,503	1,781	2,828	3,639	1,679	1,389
Additions to long-term financial liabilities	11,135	9,491	9,057	2,440	9,169	7,037	3,174
Repayment of financial liabilities	(4,841)	(4,126)	(4,612)	(5,228)	(5,073)	(3,844)	(3,035)
Dividends paid (Financial Services: incl. profit transferred from subsidiaries)	(7,572)	(6,454)	(1,267)	(746)	(589)	(491)	(479)
Proceeds from issuance of capital stock	4,782	4,076	231	231	515	176	248
Purchase of treasury stock	(198)	(169)	(1,888)	(1,570)	–	–	–
Proceeds from special distribution tax refund	1,744	1,487	–	–	–	–	–
Cash provided by (used for) financing activities	7,987	6,808	3,302	(2,045)	7,661	4,557	1,297
Effect of foreign exchange rate changes on cash and cash equivalents up to 3 months	(466)	(397)	646	351	(28)	36	24
Net increase (decrease) in cash and cash equivalents up to 3 months	(415)	(353)	1,755	(483)	(18)	376	(241)
Cash and cash equivalents (up to 3 months):							
at beginning of period	7,783	6,634	4,879	5,362	699	323	564
at end of period	7,368	6,281	6,634	4,879	681	699	323

The accompanying notes are an integral part of these Consolidated Financial Statements.

All balances have been restated from Deutsche Marks into Euros using the exchange rate as of January 1, 1999.

(Annual Report 1998 p. 70)

Exhibit 1.4   DaimlerChrysler balance sheet (annotated)

| | | 1 | | 2 | 3 | 4 | 5 | 6 | 7 |

CONSOLIDATED BALANCE SHEETS

					Consolidated At December 31,		Financial Services At December 31,	
		Note	1998 (Note 1) $	1998 €	1997 €	1998 €	1997 €
(in millions)							
1	**Assets**						
2	Intangible assets	10	3,004	2,561	2,422	104	51
3	Property, plant and equipment, net	10	34,649	29,532	28,558	53	39
4	Investments and long-term financial assets	16	3,344	2,851	2,397	632	631
5	Equipment on operating leases, net	11	17,203	14,662	11,092	12,001	9,571
6	**Fixed assets**		58,200	49,606	44,469	12,790	10,292
7	Inventories	12	13,840	11,796	10,897	654	505
8	Trade receivables	13	8,922	7,605	7,265	654	761
9	Receivables from financial services	14	31,054	26,468	21,717	26,460	21,658
10	Other receivables	15	12,642	10,775	11,376[1]	5,936	6,214
11	Securities	16	14,267	12,160	10,180	597	418
12	Cash and cash equivalents	17	7,731	6,589	6,809	681	702
13	**Current assets**		88,456	75,393	68,244	34,982	30,258
14	**Deferred taxes**	8	5,885	5,016	5,688	17	14
15	**Prepaid expenses**	19	7,197	6,134	6,430	133	71
16	Total assets (thereof short-term 1998: € 57,953; 1997: € 54,370)		159,738	136,149	124,831	47,922	40,635
17	**Liabilities and stockholders' equity**						
18	Capital stock		3,005	2,561	2,391		
19	Additional paid-in capital		8,534	7,274	2,958		
20	Retained earnings		24,091	20,533	21,892[1]		
21	Accumulated other comprehensive income		(1)	(1)	1,143		
22	Treasury stock		–	–	(424)		
23	Preferred stock		–	–	·		
24	**Stockholders' equity**	20	35,629	30,367	27,960	4,639	4,379
25	**Minority interests**		810	691	782	17	28
26	**Accrued liabilities**	22	40,629	34,629	35,787	412	508
27	Financial liabilities	23	47,436	40,430	34,375	36,810	31,381
28	Trade liabilities	24	15,074	12,848	12,026	242	90
29	Other liabilities	25	10,851	9,249	7,912	2,366	1,610
30	**Liabilities**		73,361	62,527	54,313	39,418	33,081
31	**Deferred taxes**	8	4,886	4,165	2,502	2,665	2,366
32	**Deferred income**	26	4,423	3,770	3,487	771	273
33	Total liabilities (thereof short-term 1998: € 58,181; 1997: € 50,918)		124,109	105,782	96,871	43,283	36,256
34	Total liabilities and stockholders' equity		159,738	136,149	124,831	47,922	40,635

(Annual Report 1998, p. 69)

reported in column (5). The term consolidated simply reminds us that the holding company, DaimlerChryslerAG, the legal entity, the shares of which are traded publicly is not the only company in the group. In fact it owns directly or indirectly more than 400 companies. These so called subsidiary companies are mainly owned 100%, however a few are held between 50% and 100%. We as shareholders in Daimler-Chrysler AG would learn little from analysing the financial statements of the holding company on its own. Its assets would chiefly be investments in subsidiaries, there would possibly be some debt and the only income would be dividends from subsidiaries. In order to make the financials more meaningful all the subsidiaries in the group, regardless of whether they are wholly or partially owned, are lumped together to form the consolidated or group financials. Thus all group assets are added together as are all group liabilities and all group income.

Inter-company (i.e. in the group) transactions are eliminated. Thus if the American subsidiary owes the holding company $1,000,000, this shows up as an asset on the individual holding company balance sheet and as a liability on the subsidiary balance sheet. On consolidation these two items off set. Therefore the consolidated numbers reflect the financial position and results from transactions with the world outside of the group.

In addition to the current year the company is required to report the previous year's balance sheet (1997). What is unusual in this case is that first, the company did not exist at 31 December 1997 and second, nor did the Euro. Since DaimlerChrysler AG has been formed by a pooling of interests of Daimler and Chrysler it proved quite straightforward to add together the Daimler and Chrysler balance sheets at 31 December 1997 as if they had already been merged.

If the purchase method was used the corporation would reflect only the balance sheet of the acquirer.

In order to report, in 1998, the consolidated DaimlerChrysler numbers for 1997 the following steps were required:

1 The Chrysler $-based financials are translated to a Dmark (DM) base using the $/Dm exchange rate at 31 December 1997.
2 The separate Daimler Dm financials would then be aggregated with the Chrysler Dm financials generated in (1). These consolidated accounts represent the position as if the merger took place prior to 31 December 1997.
3 The consolidated Dm financials generated in (2) are then translated into Euro at the €/Dm exchange rate on the date the Euro was invented, 1 January 1999.

Furthermore, since the Euro did not exist at midnight on 31 December 1998, the 1998 numbers were therefore translated from

Dm into Euros at the same exchange rate as in (3). The result is that both years' numbers are scaled by the same factor (Euro/Dm exchange rate at 1 January 1999) which means that the original relationship among all these numbers is retained. This will help in the ratio analysis covered in Chapter 3.

Finally, the last two columns (6 and 7) are the 1998 and 1997 balance sheets for one part of the group – financial services. Note that these numbers are in Euros (€). As with most major auto manu-facturers DaimlerChrysler AG has a division that is a sizeable bank – the numbers are reported separately for improved information content.

For the purpose of this exposition the financial services numbers will be ignored and the prime focus for the discussion will be the 1998 consolidated numbers in Euros, which of course include financial services.

The balance sheet reflects the financial position of the firm at a particular moment in time. The amounts are therefore stocks as distinct from the flows reported in the income and cash flow statements. The obvious metaphor is that of a photograph of the financial position. For this reason you will notice that the balance sheets in Exhibit 1.4 are described as '. . . at December 31'. Contrast this with the description in Exhibits 1.2 and 1.3 '. . . year ended', which implies a flow through time. Finally note that all numbers are in millions.

The most important feature of the balance sheet to grasp is the equation or identity that holds it together. In order to facilitate the discussion each line item in Exhibit 1.4 has been numbered for easy reference.

Numbers in square brackets [] refer to the line item numbers in Exhibit 1.4.

The balance sheet consists of two parts, the first headed Assets [1] and the second headed Liabilities and stockholders' equity [17]. These represent the accounting equation. Total assets [16] equal Total liabilities and stockholders' equity [34]. As the heading [17] suggests Total liabilities and stockholders' equity consists of two elements, total liabilities [33] and equity [24]. The essence of the balance sheet is now expressed in the equation shown Figure 1.1.

This is the most critical starting point in the deconstruction of a set of financials regardless of their complexity. We will often use the 'twin towers' format to depict the balance sheet as shown in Figure 1.1. In this way you can immediately see what DaimlerChrysler owns (Assets), what it owes (Liabilities) and the residual, what it owes to its shareholders (Equity). It will be immediately apparent that Daimler-Chrysler owns €136,149 in assets of which it owes €105,782 to

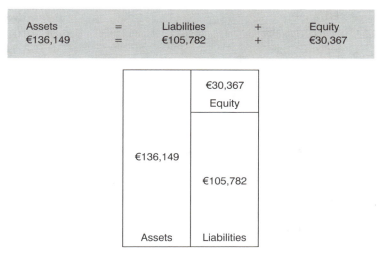

Figure 1.1   The accounting equation

various creditors. The net book value, being the difference between these of €30,367, reflects the claim of the residual claimants or shareholders. It is now clearly evident that DaimlerChrysler is about 78% debt financed, i.e. 78% of the assets are debt financed and 22% equity financed.[1]

$$\text{Debt ratio} = \frac{\text{Liabilities}}{\text{Assets}} = \frac{€105,782}{€136,149} = 77.7\%$$

The key to understanding the balance sheet is to recognize that all further analysis is simply a decomposition of the essential equation into many different sub-categories of assets, liabilities and equity.

Figure 1.4 further analyses these key numbers into various categories as displayed on the DaimlerChrysler balance sheet. The rest of this section provides a guided tour of the balance sheets by discussing each of these line items.

1.3 Assets

The assets as displayed on the DaimlerChrysler balance sheet are broken down into four major categories.

---

[1] The terms debt and liabilities are used interchangeably.

[6]	Fixed assets	49,606
[13]	Current assets	75,393
[14]	Deferred taxes	5,016
[15]	Prepaid expenses	6,134
[16]	Total assets	€136,149

1.3.1 Fixed assets

The term fixed assets refers to all those assets owned by the business that management intend to be a long-term feature of the balance sheet, i.e. usually more than one year. The definition revolves around management intention – rather than the nature of the asset. An illustration of this for DaimlerChrysler would be motor vehicles and trucks. DaimlerChrysler produces motor vehicles and trucks, the vast majority of which are built for sale, some of these are kept by the firm and used as assets in the business. The latter would be classified as fixed assets since they will be held. Whereas those intended for sale will be held as inventory under the current asset section. Thus two identical vehicles are reflected in quite different ways on the balance sheet.

It will be seen from the balance sheet that the DaimlerChrysler fixed assets are made up as follows:

[2]	Intangible assets	2,561
[3]	Property, plant and equipment, net	29,532
[4]	Investments and long-term financial assets	2,851
[5]	Equipment on operating leases, net	14,662
[6]	Fixed assets	€49,606

[2] Intangible assets	€2,561

These are assets that have no physical existence but which can have considerable value to the company. In DaimlerChrysler's case the intangible assets represent principally goodwill from the acquisition of American Motors Corporation[2] (AMC). As explained above the merger between Daimler and Chrysler does not in itself give rise to goodwill, since the merger was treated as a pooling of interests and not as an acquisition. Goodwill is the result of the acquisition of a subsidiary company by the holding company or another subsidiary in a group. It arises by default as an accounting artefact during the process of consolidation described above.

---

[2] Other intangible assets include patents, franchises and intangible pension assets.

How does goodwill arise?

Goodwill arises where the amount paid by the group for a new subsidiary to the group is in excess of the net asset value (i.e. the net equity) of that subsidiary. Let us assume that the DaimlerChrysler group company paid €10,000 for all the shares in AMC. In the balance sheet of the acquiring company (already in the group) this transaction will be recorded as an asset 'Investment in AMC €10,000'. Since the amount was paid directly to the shareholders of AMC, the AMC balance sheet is unaffected. However, at the end of the financial year when AMC is included in the group for consolidation the investment of €10,000 will be analysed into the assets and liabilities of AMC at the date of acquisition and reflected in the appropriate section of the group consolidated balance sheet. Let us suppose that the net asset value of AMC at the time of acquisition was €7,439, this would leave €2,561 unanalysed. This unanalysed amount is called goodwill and reflected in the DaimlerChrysler group balance sheet as an intangible asset under the fixed asset section. It should be noted that this remains every year as long as AMC is part of the group.

Cost of shares in AMC	10,000
Net assets (assets minus liabilities)	7,439
Goodwill	€2,561

It is useful to distinguish two distinct concepts at this stage, goodwill and the premium paid on acquisition. This is illustrated in Figure 1.2.

The premium on acquisition represents the excess paid for the investment in AMC over the market value (market capitalization) of the AMC shares immediately before acquisition. It is independent of goodwill and not accounted for anywhere, except perhaps in the books of the old shareholders of AMC, but even they are unlikely to have the shares in their balance sheet at exactly the market capitalization on the day before the announcement of the intended acquisition.

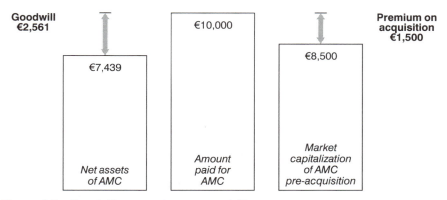

Figure 1.2 Goodwill vs premium on acquisition

How does goodwill disappear from the balance sheet?

Companies face a number of key accounting policy decisions when goodwill arises. This is organized below in Figure 1.3 which illustrates the four generic ways that goodwill is treated by companies around the world.

Figure 1.3 identifies four methods which are summarized in Table 1.1.

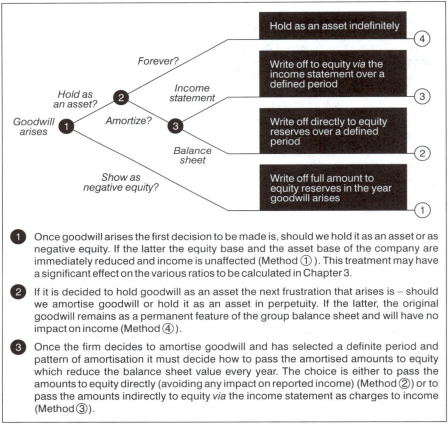

1 Once goodwill arises the first decision to be made is, should we hold it as an asset or as negative equity. If the latter the equity base and the asset base of the company are immediately reduced and income is unaffected (Method ①). This treatment may have a significant effect on the various ratios to be calculated in Chapter 3.

2 If it is decided to hold goodwill as an asset the next frustration that arises is – should we amortise goodwill or hold it as an asset in perpetuity. If the latter, the original goodwill remains as a permanent feature of the group balance sheet and will have no impact on income (Method ④).

3 Once the firm decides to amortise goodwill and has selected a definite period and pattern of amortisation it must decide how to pass the amortised amounts to equity which reduce the balance sheet value every year. The choice is either to pass the amounts to equity directly (avoiding any impact on reported income) (Method ②) or to pass the amounts indirectly to equity *via* the income statement as charges to income (Method ③).

Figure 1.3   The treatment of goodwill

Methods 1 and 2, although used quite widely around the world, are frowned upon by many accounting regulatory bodies since they are a form of so-called reserve accounting. It has only recently been ruled out in the UK without retroactive effect.

Under method 1, goodwill is swallowed up into equity as it arises whereas method 4 keeps it on the balance sheet forever. Under methods

Table 1.1   Accounting for goodwill

| | Impact on financial statements | | |
| | Balance sheet | | Income statement |
Method	Asset	Equity	Income
1 Show as negative equity	None	Reduces	No impact
2 Amortize directly to equity	Reflects goodwill as a decaying asset	Reduces with asset	No impact
3 Amortize *via* income statement	Reflects goodwill as a decaying asset	Reduces with asset	Reduces
4 Hold as an asset	Reflects total goodwill	None	None

2 and 3 the goodwill amount on the balance sheet decreases over time. Method 3 is the method most preferred and is the one adopted by DaimlerChrysler. The amount reported on the balance sheet is in fact the goodwill net of cumulative amortizations. In a schedule reported in the DaimlerChrysler annual report (not here reproduced) it is evident that the €2,561 reported is made up as follows

Full cost goodwill	4,301
Less: accumulated depreciation	1,740
Net goodwill	€2,561

The accumulated depreciation represents the amount that has been written off to the income statement on a cumulative basis. The amount for the current year was €255, which will have reduced income by this amount.

In the note 10 (not reproduced here) referred to on the balance sheet one would notice that goodwill is amortized over a period of between three and forty years. Even though a particular treatment is adopted the period over which the goodwill is depreciated can vary widely and therefore have a significant effect on the numbers reported. The methods and the impact on the various elements of the financial statements are summarized in Table 1.1.

Although these different approaches affect balance sheet and income statement items, all have the same effect on cash flow which is in the year of purchase only. However, only method 3 causes a disparity between reported net income and cash flow from operations. There are usually no taxation effects associated with the various treatments.

Does the goodwill on the balance reflect the total value of the group's goodwill?

No. The goodwill on the balance sheet relates only to purchased goodwill since the balance sheet is based essentially on the principle of historic costs. Simply put this means that only actual transactions are allowed to impact the financial statements. These transactions are recorded at transacted prices which are actual costs. Most of the goodwill associated with DaimlerChrysler has been developed by the firm, however it would only be reflected on the balance sheet of an acquirer. That is, if another company bought DaimlerChrysler and paid more than the net book value of €30,367. The goodwill in such a hypothetical transaction would be the difference between the price paid and the net book value.

A rough estimate of the total value of goodwill for DaimlerChrysler at 31 December 1998 is €53,345. This assumes that the whole of DaimlerChrysler was bought for €83,742 m, its market capitalization at 31 December 1998.

How does this difference of €53,345 between the book value of DaimlerChrysler net assets (equity) and the market value of these assets (market capitalization) actually arise?

The answer is of course that the balance sheet issued by firms does not include a number of critical, often intangible assets that have a bearing on the future cash flows of the enterprise and hence its value today.

Examples of excluded asset include; knowledge, brands, people, other intellectual property and many others, all of these assets are largely omitted from balance sheets and no attempt is made to report on these.

Therefore the historic cost balance sheet makes no attempt to value the enterprise. Its purpose is merely to be only one source of information, albeit the most important, that may be useful to those who would seek to value the firm.

The stock market on the other hand attempts to place a value on *all* of the assets. The process of establishing such a value is the central purpose of this book. The market capitalization of DaimlerChrysler at the 1998 balance sheet date was €83,742, this is based on a share price of €83.60 and 1,001.7 m shares in issue.

The difference between the book value and market value of equity can be characterized for any firm as arising from the fact that the market expects the balance sheet assets to generate a return on capital larger than a normal return. In this way there is an expectation in the forward looking market price that there will be valuable growth and the difference between book value and market value is the value of growth opportunities the firm faces. Ultimately the realization of these growth opportunities is a firm's competitive advantage.

Once realized as part of a transaction such as the acquisition of AMC, these intangibles are accounted for as goodwill.

This description draws a clear distinction between the historic cost balance sheet produced by companies and the concept of a value-based balance sheet which is essential for decision making. This concept of a value-based balance sheet is introduced in Chapter 5.

The historic balance sheet is a backward looking document in as far as it reflects transactions that have already taken place. Whereas a value-based balance sheet attempts to look at the future and comprehensively value all of a firm's assets.

[3] Property, plant and equipment, net	€29,532

The next category of fixed asset we encounter is property, plant and equipment. Property, plant and equipment represents those assets not intended for sale that are used continuously to manufacture, display, store and transport DaimlerChrysler products. The amount includes land, buildings, machinery, equipment, furniture, vehicles and other assets.

Generally these assets are reflected on the balance sheet at cost less accumulated depreciation, hence the term net.

In a separate schedule (not reproduced here) in the DaimlerChrysler financial statements the following is reported.

Gross cost of property, plant and equipment	65,937
Less: Accumulated depreciation	36,405
Property, plant and equipment, net	€29,532

As with goodwill, the number displayed for plant and equipment is not intended to reflect their market value or indicate the cost of replacing these assets.

Depreciation is the process whereby the cost of a fixed asset is allocated to the profit and loss (income statement), and therefore equity, over its useful life. Management have some discretion over the choice of useful life and the pattern of write down, which is usually on a straight line basis. This means that the total cost of the asset is written down in equal amounts in each year of its useful life. Other patterns are in use. The gross amount reflects the original cost, accumulated depreciation reflects that part of the original cost which has already been written down and passed through the income statement as a cost and so has reduced equity in this amount. The net amount reflects the residual of the original costs still remaining to be depreciated in future years.

The total depreciation charge in the 1998 financial year for DaimlerChrysler was €7,331 – this is a non-cash item and therefore causes income and cash flow from operations to be different. This is identical to the impact of amortizing goodwill.

The term depletion is usually used in the mining and extractive sectors. Since DaimlerChrysler is not active in this sector the term is not encountered.

[4]   Investments and long-term financial assets   €2,851

The next category of fixed asset reported is that of financial investments. This tells us that management have invested in various financial investments including shares in other companies, government bonds and loans to other companies. Notice that where shares are purchased in other companies the percentage holding by group companies must be less than 50% to be classified as an investment[3]. If the holding is greater than 50% the investee company is usually deemed to be a subsidiary. As discussed above subsidiaries are consolidated into the group balance sheet and therefore do not appear as investments in the group consolidated balance sheet.

We will also encounter financial investments in the current asset section of the balance sheet – as in our example of motor vehicles above, there is no economic difference between the investments identified as fixed assets and those marketable securities classified as current assets. The distinction is based entirely on management's intention *vis-à-vis* holding period.

The investments are also implicitly part of the balance sheet that the management, in effect, manages passively on behalf of their shareholders. Since it represents capital raised on the capital market as debt and equity which is now passed back into the capital market, the process raises questions about the value added by management to this capital.

Investments are long-term financial assets classified as fixed assets and reported at their cost. They are not subject to depreciation or amortization, but they will be written down to market value if this falls below cost for a sustained period. The write down is similar in nature to depreciation in that it passes through the income statement as a cost and so reduces equity. Like depreciation these write downs do not affect cash flow.

[5]   Equipment on operating leases, net   €14,662

The final type of fixed asset we encounter is equipment on operating leases.

---

[3] In certain circumstances holdings below 50% are classified as a subsidiary if management have effective control.

This represents, chiefly, automobiles and commercial vehicles manufactured by the group that are leased to others on a long-term basis. The vehicles are therefore owned by DaimlerChrysler but used by others who pay a rental fee for the use thereof.

Although these are likely to have passed from inventory in one subsidiary and sold at a profit to another that arranges the leases, any profit on the intra-group transaction is reversed on consolidation and the assets are recorded at cost to the group. These assets are depreciated in the same way as plant and equipment and reported net of accumulated depreciation.

In a separate schedule (not reproduced here) the following information was available.

Gross cost of equipment and operating leases	18,225
Less: Accumulated depreciation	3,563
Equipment on operating leases, net	€14,662

1.3.2 Current assets

We now come to the second category of asset reported by Daimler-Chrysler, current assets.

Current assets are all those assets and claims owned by the firm that are expected to be turned into cash in the foreseeable future, usually during the next financial year. Although current assets as a category is a permanent feature of a firm's balance sheet the constituents are continuously revolving, i.e. being turned into cash and new short-term assets. Current assets constitute a considerable portion of DaimlerChrysler capital (55.4%) and therefore it is imperative that these assets are effectively managed to ensure that the overall return on capital is adequate.

DaimlerChrysler's current assets are made up as follows:

[7]	Inventories	11,796
[8]	Trade receivables	7,605
[9]	Receivables from financial services	26,468
[10]	Other receivables	10,775
[11]	Securities	12,160
[12]	Cash and cash equivalents	6,589
[13]	Current assets	€75,393

[7] Inventories	€11,796

The inventory of an auto manufacturer such as DaimlerChrysler consists of three main categories; raw material to be used in the manufacturing process; work in process or partially finished goods and finished goods. Around 60% of DaimlerChrysler inventory is finished goods. The inventories are carried on the balance sheet at cost and include all direct cost of producing the items on hand at the year end. This includes materials and direct labour. The determination of the cost of inventory has an important impact on the level of profit. Since the total direct cost of production for the year is allocated between cost of sales (charge to income) and inventory (hold on the balance sheet) any amount allocated to inventory constitutes a diversion of costs from the P&L to be temporarily held in the balance sheet. This has the effect of increasing profits in the current year, however in the following year the costs will find their way into the income statement as the items are sold. Thus a sustained pattern of inflating the cost of inventory has the effect of boosting profits and the asset base.

There are two main methods of costing inventory being used at DaimlerChrysler; the so-called first-in-first-out (FIFO) method which assumes that inventory on hand is the freshest, and the last-in-first-out (LIFO) method which assumes that inventory on hand is the oldest possible. Since direct costs are usually rising, FIFO-costed inventory is usually higher than LIFO-costed inventory. This means that FIFO-based profits are higher. Although the methods impact income in different ways and have different inventory holding values on the balance sheet, there is no direct impact on cash flow from operations. However, if the two bases are accepted for tax purposes, LIFO-based profits, being lower, will result in lower taxes being paid.

If all of DaimlerChrysler's inventory had been valued on a FIFO-basis, inventory would have been higher by €549. This amount is not recognized on the balance sheet and it represents a LIFO reserve, that is the cumulative effect of the difference in the two methods. The impact on the current year's income of adopting the LIFO method for costing some of its inventory was €2 m.

[8] Trade receivables	€7,605

The next current asset we find is trade receivables. The financial statements recognize a sale at the time of delivery of the product. Thus once a vehicle leaves inventory it is recorded as a sale, even though it may not have been paid for by the customer. Therefore at the time of drawing up the balance sheet any amounts still outstanding that have already been included in the sales are carried as trade receivables.

Obviously, the longer it takes to collect the money due from customers the longer the firm is without the cash. Thus accounts receivable represent another major absorption of capital which does not generate a cash return directly.

In the case of DaimlerChrysler, the amount of trade receivables represents amounts owed by trade customers, mainly distributors. The amount shown is net of a deduction for doubtful debts.

The actual amount owed to DaimlerChrysler by trade customers is €8,462, however an allowance of €857 for doubtful debts has been deducted.

Gross trade receivables	8,462
Less: Allowance for doubtful debts	857
Trade receivables	€7,605

This allowance of 10% is rather conservative by international standards, however it is a matter for management policy and will be influenced by management's past experiences with the recovery of receivables. The net figure displayed on the balance sheet is intended to reflect the amount management expects to receive.

Notice that trade receivables are recorded at selling price and therefore include the profit on the items sold.

[9] Receivables from financial services	€26,468

Receivables from financial services are distinct from trade receivables in that DaimlerChrysler Financial Services provides explicit financing arrangements to retail customers, whereas trade receivables are charged on invoice.

The financial arrangements are of two types, instalment sale and financial lease. The two contracts have different legal and tax implications but economically they amount to the customer paying off the car in stages and since they are in effect borrowing from the company a financial charge is levied.

DaimlerChrysler will have raised the sale at cash sales price and reflected this amount in financial receivables. As the instalment or lease payments are received in cash they are split into a capital and a financial (interest) element, the former goes to reduce receivables, the latter is reflected as revenue from financial services.

It turns out from further disclosures in the annual report that €14,733 of these receivables are due after more than one year.

[10] Other receivables	€10,775

Other receivables represent amounts owed to the group other than by trade customers and from financial services. This includes amounts owed by affiliated and related companies that are not consolidated. It also includes short-term net traded investments. The amount shown is net of a bad debt allowance of 10%.

[11] Securities	€12,160

This represents the marketable securities owned by the group. An extraordinarily large amount of excess cash has been invested in liquid assets including debt and equity investments. This along with the cash in the bank represents a considerable 'war chest' of financial capacity. It does give management considerable flexibility, however, it raises questions on the ability of management to add value to this capital as it is simply reinvested in the capital markets from where it came. These are important issues in the process of value creation and corporate policy which will be addressed later in the book. These investments are usually carried at the lower cost or market. However, where securities are available for sale they are reported at market even if higher than cost. The unrealized gain from such revaluations is not recognized in income but held in a special comprehensive income reserve (see section 1.4.1).

[12] Cash and cash equivalents	€6,589

Cash is as you would expect notes and coins in petty cash and deposits with banks. Cash equivalents are money market instruments such as deposits with a maturity of less than three months.

Taking item [11] and [12] together DaimlerChrysler holds cash and marketable securities of €18,749, in liquid money which is quite an extraordinary amount. There are no non-financial quoted companies in the UK and US that hold as much in cash and marketable securities. This reflects a very different tradition and is our first encounter with the major differences between Anglo-American and Rhenish corporate governance to which we will make reference again. Does holding so much cash really create value? This is a question being asked by the shareholders of many European companies.

A consequence of the large cash and marketable securities position is that a significant financial income is generated and reflected in the income statement.

1.3.3 Other assets

This guided tour of the asset side of the DaimlerChrysler balance sheet concludes with a description of these last two items.

[14] Deferred taxes	€5,016

Deferred taxes are included in total assets but as neither a current nor as a fixed asset. Similarly it will noticed that on the other side of the balance sheet there is a line item which is also called deferred taxes [31] which is included in total liabilities.

Deferred tax as an asset has arisen in DaimlerChrysler from the existence of 'NOLs' in some subsidiaries of the group. 'NOLs' or net operating losses mean that the losses in these companies will act as a tax shield on future income. In the US these are called 'tax credit carry forwards'. If a group company has a loss for tax purposes it does not receive a rebate from the tax authorities, it is usually allowed to reduce subsequent years income (if any) by the loss carried forward. The result of this is that the firm's effective tax rate will look higher, than the marginal corporate tax rate in the year the 'NOL' arises and lower when it is used up. Here in Table 1.2a is a numerical example of how this arises.

Table 1.2a   Illustration of the effect of NOLs on effective tax rates

Without deferred tax adjustment	Profitable subsidiaries	Non-profitable subsidiaries	Group total	%
Year 1				
Income (loss)	10,000	(2,000)	8,000	100
Taxes actually paid @56%	(5,600)	0	(5,600)	70
Income (loss) after tax	4,400	(2,000)	2,400	30
Year 2				
Income	10,000	2,000	12,000	100
Taxes actually paid @56%	(5,600)	0	(5,600)	47
Income after tax	4,400	2,000	6,400	53

The income (loss) reported in each year is assumed to be taxable. Taxes are calculated at the rate of 56% (this is the German marginal corporate tax rate to which DaimlerChrysler is subject). Since the loss incurred by a particular subsidiary has no tax effect, i.e. no credit is given against other subsidiaries taxes due – the group's effective tax rate is shown to be 70%. However this NOL of €2,000 is available as a deduction against subsequent income. In the example the non-profitable subsidiary in year one turns in a profit of €2,000 in year 2. Since this will not be taxed because of the NOL brought forward the group effective tax rate is now 47%. Thus NOLs increase the effective tax rate when they arise and decrease it when they reverse. This is so because the NOL gives rise to a so-called timing difference between the reported income and the taxable income. In this case the reported income recognized the loss in the subsidiary in the year it arises whereas the tax authorities recognize the costs only when there is taxable income in a subsequent year.

Timing differences give rise to a fluctuation in effective tax rates since there is a mis-match between the tax line and the income line in the income statement.

The financial statements of DaimlerChrysler and virtually all other companies are based on the principle of matching whereby costs are matched to the revenues to which they relate. This principle dictates that an adjustment should be made to the reported taxes to rectify this mis-match which arises due to the timing difference caused by events such as NOLs. Table 1.2b illustrates the mechanics of the deferred tax adjustments resulting from NOLs.

Table 1.2b   Illustration of the effect of deferred tax adjustments resulting from NOLs

With deferred tax adjustments	Profitable subsidiaries	Non-profitable subsidiaries	Group total	%	Cumulative balance
Year 1					
Income (loss)	10,000	(2,000)	8,000	100	
Taxes actually paid @56%	(5,600)		(5,600)		
Deferred tax credit	–	1,120	1,120		1120
Total tax charge	(5,600)	1,120	(4,480)	56	
Income (loss) after tax	4,400	(880)	3,520	44	
Year 2					
Income	10,000	2,000	12,000	100	
Taxes actually paid @56%	(5,600)		(5,600)		
Deferred tax charge	–	(1,120)	(1,120)		0
Total tax charge	(5,600)	(1,120)	(6,720)	56	
Income after tax	4,400	880	5,280	44	

The matching principle underlying deferred tax adjustments has the effect, as illustrated, of reporting a constant tax rate in each year. There are two other effects. First, the reported tax line is no longer a cash based item, it consists of taxes actually paid and an accounting adjustment which does not affect cash flow. Second, the cumulative effects of these income statement adjustments are held on the balance sheet as deferred taxes. In the case illustrated, since the tax charge is being reduced in the first year, the deferred tax appears as an asset on the balance sheet.

Timing differences can work the other way, that is, where the tax charge is increased in earlier years and reduced in subsequent years. The most common example of this is where fiscal authorities permit firms to write off assets more quickly than the period assumed for financial reporting. Therefore revenue in the early part of an asset's life is shielded from taxes which are deferred to later years. This timing difference is illustrated in Table 1.3a. Here we assume an asset, costing €4,000 in year 1, to be written off over two years (straight line) for financial reporting but allowed to be written off in one year for tax purposes.

Table 1.3a   Illustration of the effect of timing differences caused by depreciation

Without deferred tax adjustment	Financial reporting	%	Tax assessment	%
Year 1				
Income before depreciation	12,000		12,000	
Depreciation	(2,000)		(4,000)	
Income before tax	10,000	100	8,000	
Tax, actually paid @56%	(4,480)	44.8	4,480	56
Income after tax	5,520			
Year 2				
Income before depreciation	12,000		12,000	
Depreciation	(2,000)		0	
Income before tax	10,000	100	12,000	
Tax, actually paid @56%	(6,720)	67	(6,720)	56
Income after tax	3,280			

In this case the effective tax rate reported is 44.8% in year 1 and 67% in year 2. The timing difference arises in year 1 when the fiscal authorities allow the full write off of the asset thus reducing taxes payable. However, in year 2 the asset is fully depreciated for tax purposes and an apparently higher effective tax rate is reported. Table 1.3b illustrates how the deferred tax adjustment would work.

Notice how the deferred tax adjustments smooth the income reported, reporting the same income after tax each year as opposed to a fluctuating amount without deferred tax. As with our example of the NOL timing difference the reported effective tax rate is equal to the

Table 1.3b Illustration of the effect of deferred tax adjustment resulting from depreciation

With deferred tax adjustments	Financial reporting	%	Cumulative deferred tax on balance sheet	Tax assessment	%
Year 1					
Income before depreciation	12,000			12,000	
Depreciation	(2,000)			(4,000)	
Income before tax	10,000	100		8,000	
Taxes paid @56%	(4,480)			4,480	56
Deferred tax charge	(1,120)		(1,120)		
Tax reported	(5,600)	56			
Income after tax	4,400				
Year 2					
Income before depreciation	12,000			12,000	
Depreciation	(2,000)			0	
Income before tax	10,000	100		12,000	
Taxes paid @56%	(6,720)			6,720	56
Deferred tax credit	1,120		0		
Tax reported	(5,600)	56			
Income after tax	4,400				

firm's marginal tax rate of 56%. In this case notice how in year one the tax reported is more than the taxes paid and *vice versa* in year 2.

Again the tax reported consists of a cash paid element and an accounting adjustment. However, in this case the balance sheet reflects a deferred tax liability at the end of year 1.

It is quite unusual to report deferred tax assets and deferred tax liabilities separately on the face of the balance sheet. Although, by doing so DaimlerChrysler have boosted their total reported assets by €4,165. This represents the amount of deferred tax liabilities [31] reported on the liability section of the balance sheet. Later in this chapter we will rearrange the balance sheet in preparation for further analysis. One of the adjustments will be to set off these two items. Thus deferred taxes will be reported on a net basis as follows:

[14]	Deferred tax (asset)	5,016
[31]	Deferred tax (liability)	4,165
	Deferred tax (net asset)	€851

In summary deferred tax adjustments:

1 are based on the accounting principle of matching;
2 create a non-cash component of taxes reported on the income statement;
3 smooth earnings over time;
4 remove the effect of timing differences on taxes paid and taxes reported;
5 give rise to deferred tax assets (such as NOLs) and deferred tax liabilities.

Are deferred tax assets/liabilities real and do they increase/decrease the value of the firm?

The liabilities are not legal liabilities, they are not payable, no interest is incurred and they are contingent on future income. If you are selling a firm you would probably suggest that deferred tax liabilities are an accounting artefact. However, if you were buying a firm you might argue that these balances reflect tax allowances already used up which will mean that future revenues will be taxed at a higher rate. Similarly, deferred tax assets do not generate a direct return although they are valuable in as far as they represent tax shields against future revenues. These items actually do reveal something about the future after tax cash flows of the business and therefore are relevant for valuation. It is not quite as simple as adding or deducting the amount on the balance sheet. More on this later.

[15] Prepaid expenses	€6,134

The final item on the asset section of the balance sheet is prepaid expenses. DaimlerChrysler makes no distinction on the face of the balance sheet between long-term and short-term prepaid expenses.

Prepaid expenses represent amounts paid in advance of the service or benefit being received. This usually involves relatively small amounts such as insurance premiums paid for cover that extends beyond the current year. Again this illustrates the principle of matching. The expenditure has been incurred this year but held over to be charged against revenue in the following year to which it is matched. The €6,134 described as prepaid expenses includes an interesting transaction arising from the merger. Immediately before the merger the Chrysler Corporation issued shares to the Chrysler employee pension fund (an entity quite separate from Chrysler). The transaction involved no cash. There was an increase in equity (see below) and this required an increase in the asset side of the equation. The amount is included as a prepaid pension cost which will be passed back to equity (retained earnings (see below)) through the income statement as pension costs over a number of years[4]. There were other prepaid pension costs as well, in total €5,309 relate to prepaid pension costs.

Prepaid expenses have a counterpart in the liability section of the balance sheet – deferred income. This represents amounts that have been received by the group in advance of the services or benefits being delivered. Again, as part of the rearrangement of items the short-term element of prepaid expenses will be shown as a current asset.

[15]	Prepaid expenses	6,134
	Less: Short-term element	854
	Prepaid expenses long term	€5,280

1.3.4 Summary of the asset section

This concludes the guided tour of the asset section of the balance sheet. We have encountered three fundamental accounting concepts that underlie the preparation of financial statements. They are:

1 *The historic cost convention*
   All items in the financial statement are based on actual transactions and recorded at the prices at the time of the transaction. These items on the balance sheet are typically left at this historic cost even if prices in markets have moved on and these assets have quite different values.
2 *The principle of matching*
   Costs and revenues that are related are recognized in the same period even if the transactions are incomplete. An example of this is deferred taxation.
3 *The prudence concept*
   The financial statements are drawn up on the principle of conservatism thus costs are anticipated and revenues are typically not.

The implications of these principles are:

1 Assets on the balance sheet do not reflect their value or replacement cost.
2 Cash flow and income are not the same.
3 Certain assets do not appear on the balance sheet.

Our attention now moves to the liability section of the balance sheet.

---

[4] This cost is borne by all shareholders in the new company and therefore has considerable implications for the terms of the deal.

1.4 Total liabilities and stockholders' equity

The other side of DaimlerChrysler accounting equation is represented by liabilities and stockholders' equity made up as follows:

[24]	Stockholders' equity	30,367
[33]	Total liabilities	105,782
[34]	Total liabilities and stockholders' equity	€136,149

This constitutes the next section of the balance sheet. We will now describe each item as it appears in the balance sheet.

1.4.1 Stockholders' equity

[24] Stockholders' equity	€30,367

This item is the total equity interest that all stockholders have in the firm. It represents the net worth of the enterprise being total assets minus total liabilities. In this sense it is known as the net asset value or the residual interest of stockholders. The stockholders are the ultimate owners of the enterprise, although their claim on the assets is subordinate to the other claimants or creditors, i.e. represented by total liabilities. Therefore if a firm becomes insolvent (i.e. its liabilities exceeds its assets), the equity becomes negative and the other liabilities would have to be settled ahead of the shareholders. The concept of limited liability ensures that the shareholders would not have to stand in for the deficit. Happily the shareholders of Daimler-Chrysler currently enjoy a considerable positive claim on the assets of the business. The equity section is analysed into different categories for legal and accounting reasons. On the DaimlerChrysler balance sheet we observe the following:

[18]	Capital stock	2,561
[19]	Additional paid-in capital	7,274
[20]	Retained earnings	20,533
[21]	Accumulated other comprehensive income	(1)
[22]	Treasury stock	0
[23]	Preferred stock	0
[24]	Stockholders' equity	€30,367

[18] Capital stock	€2,561

In the broadest sense capital stock represents shares in the owner-ship of the business. In the case of DaimlerChrysler it represents

1,001,733,220 registered ordinary shares of no par value. Capital stock usually represents the nominal value of the ordinary share capital, where these shares have a par value, and the total paid in capital where the shares are of no par value. The nominal (par) value is the monetary amount written on the share certificate. This amount has no particular economic meaning and shares are usually issued (i.e. sold by the company) for amounts above the par value. The amount received by the company above the par value also forms part of the share capital but is classified as additional paid in capital or as share premium. In most countries there are restrictions on how these items may be accounted for subsequently.

As a result of the merger of Daimler and Chrysler *via* the pooling of interest method shareholders in the two companies relinquished their old shares and received new shares. The new shares are of no par value but the old shares did have a par value. Therefore the capital stock line represents the original par value of the capital paid in, which represents a par value of €2.56 per new share.

Another significant feature of the DaimlerChrysler shares is that they are registered. Most German companies have bearer shares which means that the identity of the shareholder is anonymous. Daimler had bearer shares and Chrysler registered shares (standard US practice) – and although the firm is headquartered in Germany and is registered as a German owned AG (Aktiengesellschaft) it has adopted the Anglo-American practice of registered shares.

[19] Additional paid-in capital   €7,274

The additional paid-in capital is the amount paid by the shareholders over and above the original par value of the shares, i.e. above €2.56 per new share. In the case of many commonwealth countries this amount is known as share premium.

There is no economic distinction between capital stock and additional paid-in capital, together they represent the accumulative amount of cash originally paid into the company by shareholders.

In short these items represent the permanent capital of the business which is not distributable as dividends. Although from time to time companies may repurchase some of their shares under certain conditions, which vary from country to country.

[20] Retained earnings   €20,533

At its inception a company has no retained earnings. Retained earnings accumulate as the company earns profits and reinvests or 'retains' profits in the business. Retained earnings represent the accumulated profits since the start of the business less the accumulated dividends paid.

It represents the increase in the net assets of the business, from trading, for the benefit of shareholders, not yet paid out.

You will notice that the DaimlerChrysler retained earnings number decreased during the year by €1,359.

Retained earnings at 31 December 1997	21,892
Retained earnings at 31 December 1998	20,533
Reduction in retained earnings	€1,359

This occurred because DaimlerChrysler paid out more dividends than it had earnings during the 1998 financial year. This was chiefly due to a special distribution of €5,284 to the old Daimler shareholders as part of the merger agreement.

The retained earnings also represent the amount of dividends that could be legally distributed.

Under the German corporate law (Aktiengesetz) the amount of dividends available for distribution to shareholders is based on the earnings of DaimlerChrysler AG (the parent company only) as reported in its statutory financial statements determined in accordance with the German Commercial code (Handlegesetzbuch).

There is often confusion on the economic meaning of retained earnings and other reserves. It is tempting to assume that the retained earnings and the other reserves of the business are locked away in a bank safe as money, immediately available for distribution to shareholders.

In section 1.3.2 it was noted how well DaimlerChrysler is endowed with cash and yet the €6,589 reported as cash is considerably less than the amount in retained earnings. This is so because the retained earning have been invested in many assets. Therefore, although a company may have considerable retained earnings and reserves it does not follow that there is the liquidity available to be able to distribute these to shareholders. In fact if there were liquid assets available to such an extent shareholders could legitimately question the implications for the future growth of the business.

[21] Accumulated other comprehensive income	€(1)

This amount in brackets means it is to be deducted from the other elements of the shareholders' equity. This line item represents the very latest innovation in accounting. Previously these were transactions and accounting effects that affected the reported value of assets and liabilities but which were not dealt with in the income statement and therefore were not included in retained earnings on the balance sheet. This item constitutes an accounting reserve which is a 'catch all' for adjustments not recognized in income. In the case of DaimlerChrysler, as with any global company, the account is made up chiefly of large currency translation adjustments. This is the amount by which non-monetary assets and liabilities change primarily as a result of changes in exchange rates. For example an item of plant held in the US at the end of 1997 at $1,000,000 would be reflected in the DaimlerChrysler accounts as €913,000 whereas this same item would be reflected in the 1998 numbers as €852,000. The difference is classified as a translation loss and it is not reflected in the income statement but shown as part of the accumulated other comprehensive income reserve. The amounts in this example arise as shown in Table 1.4.

Table 1.4   Currency translation loss

Date	Asset amount	Dm/$	DM	€/Dm	€
31/12/97	1,000,000 @	1.79 Dm	1,790,000	0,51	913,000
31/12/98	1,000,000 @	1.67 Dm	1,670,000	0,51	852,000
Translation currency loss					61,000

Even though no transaction has taken place it is necessary to include the American fixed assets in the consolidated numbers which means that although the $ amount is constant the rate at which these are translated for reporting in Euro has changed during the year and a loss is recognized. Notice that the loss arises because during 1998 the $ weakened against the Dm. Since the Dm is translated into € at the same rate in both years there is no additional effect. In future the translation gains and losses will be determined by the fluctuation in the exchange rate between the $ and €. Since the creation of the Euro in January 1998 the Euro has generally weakened against the dollar which means that American assets reported in € balance sheets will give rise to translation gains.

The current year translation loss for DaimlerChrysler was €1,402 which is why accumulated other comprehensive income has reduced by so much. This loss has reversed all previous translation gains. (This information was available in footnotes to the accounts.) Conversely it should be noted that adjustments relating to transactions which are executed in currencies other than the Euro are included as gains or losses in the income statement.

In addition DaimlerChrysler had a small unrealized gain due to the revaluation of available for sale securities in the manner described in section 1.3.2.

[22] Treasury Stock	0

If a company repurchases or 'buys back' its own shares, these purchased shares are reported as treasury stock and are deducted from equity. Notice the 1997 number for treasury stock is (€424). The brackets indicating a deduction from the other equity items.

Since at the end of 1998 treasury stock is recorded at zero we know that this stock must have been re-issued, so they disappear from the balance sheet. We will encounter this transaction in the cash flow statement in Chapter 2.

[23] Preferred stock	0

Although DaimlerChrysler does not have any preferred stock in issue (and hence the value is zero) it is authorized to issue this type of stock which is why it reports a line item preferred stock.

These shares are quite common and enjoy some preference over ordinary shares with respect to dividends and in the distribution of assets in case of liquidation. These shares usually have a par value and indicate the dividends payable as a percentage of par value. Unlike with debt the company can pay the dividend only if there is an appropriate level of profit and reserves available. However, they are usually cumulative which means that if a dividend is missed the amount owed is accumulated year on year in preference over ordinary dividends. They may be redeemable or non-redeemable. This means that in certain cases the capital will be repaid within a specific period or not at all. If the latter they remain as permanent capital and would usually be convertible on specific terms to ordinary shares. The dividend on preference shares is not deductible for tax purposes in contrast to interest on debt.

1.4.2 Total liabilities

We now turn to the final element in the accounting equation, total liabilities, which represent the amount owed by the company to claimants other than shareholders. This section of the balance sheet consists of six elements.

[25]	Minority interests	691
[26]	Accrued liabilities	34,629
[30]	Liabilities	62,527
[31]	Deferred taxes	4,165
[32]	Deferred income	3,770
[33]	Total liabilities (short term €58,181)	€105,782

DaimlerChrysler have adopted an unusual display pattern for their liabilities. They do not report a current and a long-term section as separate amounts. It will be noted that the short-term element is reported unusually as what amounts to a footnote as €58,181. However, it takes much investigation in the footnotes to assign this amount to the various categories of liabilities reported. Later in the chapter we will be rearranging the display as a basis for further analysis and a separate section for short-term liabilities will be created on the face of the balance sheet.

[25] Minority interests	**€691**

In the section above on the introduction to the balance sheet the process of consolidation was explained. It was pointed out that all the assets and liabilities of the group's subsidiaries are added together regardless of whether they are wholly owned. If any subsidiary is less than 100% held the share not held by the group is held by stockholders who collectively own less than 50% of the subsidiary and are therefore described as minority interests. Minority interests on a balance sheet therefore represent the aggregate share of these outside stockholders in the equity of all subsidiaries that are not wholly owned. Since we will have included all the assets and liabilities the accounting equation would not hold if these residual claims of minorities were not reported.

The minority interest does give rise to some difficulties of classification. Since it is legally equity, in that the amount does not have to be paid back, and since interest is not payable one may be inclined to classify it as equity. However, it is not our (the holding company shareholders) equity and as such represents other people's money or outside funds. Thus it is usually shown as any other liability. The amount in the case of DaimlerChrysler is small which suggests that the group tends to have wholly owned subsidiaries. We will encounter a similar caption in the income statement which arises for the same reasons, and the treatment of which will be dealt with as a finance charge for symmetry.

[26] Accrued liabilities	€34,629

In the asset section of the balance sheet we encountered an item – prepaid expenses. This represented amounts that were already paid which were not yet due and were therefore held over to be charged to future years' income statements. The accrued liability is the liability counterpart of prepaid expenses. Here the amount in question has not been paid but is anticipated as a cost and held over on the balance sheet in the liability section until it is paid. Therefore this item has been realized by a book-keeping entry and reflects those accumulated costs that have been accrued but are not yet due for payment in cash. The single largest amount included for DaimlerChrysler is related to pension liabilities.

It is usual practice to describe the short-term element of accrued liabilities as accrued expenses and report it in the current liability section of the balance sheet. In a footnote to the DaimlerChrysler financial statements the breakdown between short-term and long-term accrued liabilities is given.

[26] Accrued liabilities	34,629
Less: Long-term accrued liabilities	22,424
Short-term accrued liabilities (accrued expenses)	€12,205

Other accrued liabilities include such items as personnel cost accrued, income taxes accrued and restructuring costs. Interest is not payable on accrued liabilities.

[30] Liabilities	€62,527

This item reflects the debt that DaimlerChrysler owes and it is made up as follows:

[27] Financial liabilities	40,430
[28] Trade liabilities	12,848
[29] Other liabilities	9,249
[30] Liabilities	€62,527

[27] Financial liabilities	€40,430

The financial liabilities show how much DaimlerChrysler owes on specific debt contracts – all of these require interest to be paid at different rates and there are a variety of liabilities. The breakdown between short-term (due within one year) and long-term is reported in the footnotes as follows:

[27]	Financial liabilities	40,430
	Less: Long-term portion	19,955
	Short term portion	€20,475

There is a wide variety of different types of debt on DaimlerChrysler's balance sheet, some with fixed interest rates and some with variable. In addition some of the debt is convertible into equity. This means that DaimlerChrysler has borrowed money, probably at lower than market interest rates, whereby the holder of this debt is able to convert the debt into shares at pre-specified conversion rates over a specified period. The holder of such convertible debt has an instrument that is one part debt and one part call option. Since the option is valuable the debt usually attracts a lower than market rate of interest.

The major implication of the existence of convertible debt is that there is a potential dilution of future earnings per share – in that the number of shares in issue would increase on conversion. We will encounter this when we deal with the calculations of earnings per share in the next chapter.

[28] Trade liabilities	€12,848

In the same way that DaimlerChrysler does not get paid by their customers on delivery so too does DaimlerChrysler not pay its suppliers immediately. Although goods and services may have been delivered and used during the year some have yet to be paid for at the year end. Thus the costs are recognized but the liability remains much like we saw with accrued expenses. Although interest is not directly payable on these accounts it is likely that the expenses will be recorded at prices that may reflect some implied interest charges. Suppliers will usually offer better prices for cash payments. These foregone discounts really represents a finance cost, however, they are accounted for along with the cost of goods and services.

[29] Other liabilities	€9,249

This item represents loans that are interest bearing owed to affiliated companies – not consolidated. These are economically no different from other financial liabilities.

[31] Deferred taxes	€4,165

Deferred taxes were discussed in section 1.3.3 and this discussion included deferred tax liabilities. It was suggested that these liabilities should be set off to deferred assets for display purposes.

[32] Deferred income	€3,770

In the same way that expenses paid in advance are held back from the income statement as an asset on the balance sheet, income received (either as cash or as recognized in the value of asset) in advance is held back from the income statement and retained on the balance sheet as a liability.

Financial income on certain financial receivables have a component of deferred income.

It is common practice to set off prepaid expenses and deferred income.

This concludes a rather extensive tour of the balance sheet.

Before moving on to the other two reports that make up the financial statements, let us consider how the DaimlerChrysler balance sheet might be rearranged to a format that would be helpful for further analysis.

1.5 Reconstructing the balance sheet for further analysis

The twin towers format of the balance sheet is reproduced in Figure 1.4 with the analysis of the various items displayed on the face of the DaimlerChrysler report. The assets are first broken down to form categories including fixed and current. These two classes are further analysed into the various items reported. The other side of the balance sheet analyses equity and debt. The equity analysis has grouped the capital stock and additional paid-in capital as reported on the original

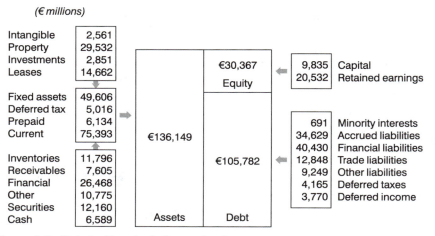

(€ millions)

Intangible	2,561			
Property	29,532			
Investments	2,851	€30,367	9,835	Capital
Leases	14,662	Equity	20,532	Retained earnings
Fixed assets	49,606			
Deferred tax	5,016			
Prepaid	6,134		691	Minority interests
Current	75,393	€136,149	34,629	Accrued liabilities
			40,430	Financial liabilities
Inventories	11,796	€105,782	12,848	Trade liabilities
Receivables	7,605		9,249	Other liabilities
Financial	26,468		4,165	Deferred taxes
Other	10,775		3,770	Deferred income
Securities	12,160			
Cash	6,589	Assets	Debt	

Figure 1.4   DaimlerChrysler balance sheet

balance sheet as one item on the diagram, described as capital. Similarly, the retained earnings and accumulated other comprehensive income items have been added together and described as retained earnings. The debt is analysed into the seven items as they appear on the original balance sheet.

Presenting the balance sheet in the form of a diagram is designed to facilitate the adjustments that will improve the analysis.

The DaimlerChrysler adopted layout is quite different from an Anglo American style balance sheet, although perfectly adequate it does not provide an immediate starting point for analysis. The following adjustments are made to the balance sheet in Figure 1.4 to produce the balance sheet in Figure 1.5.

1. Set off deferred tax assets and liabilities
As indicated earlier it is unusual to separate deferred tax assets and liabilities. The €4,165 deferred tax item in liabilities is removed and the deferred tax asset of €5,016 is reduced by this amount. The net deferred tax asset is thus €851.

2. Transfer prepaid expenses to accrued liabilities
The bulk of the prepaid expenses are with respect to pension costs and the same is true for accrued liabilities. It is more usual to group these line items. Thus the prepaid expenses line on the asset side is removed (€6,134) and the accrued liabilities are reduced by the same amount, this ensures that the equation continues to hold and the balance sheet 'balances'.

3. Reclassify deferred income with accrued liabilities

It is usual to classify accounting accruals and deferrals together. Thus deferred income is reduced by €3,770 to zero and accrued liabilities increases correspondingly. This adjustment does not affect the amount of total assets.

The combined effect on accrued liabilities of adjustments (2) and (3) is as follows:

Accrued liabilities per Figure 1.4	34,629
Less: pre-paid expenses (adjustment 2)	(6,134)
Add: deferred income (adjustment 3)	3,770
Total accrued liabilities per Figure 1.5	€32,265

4. Disaggregate long-term and current liabilities

DaimlerChrysler chose to make no distinction between the current and long-term element of each item in the liabilities section of the balance sheet. However, the aggregate amount of current liabilities was reported in brackets in line [33] as €58,181. Using information supplied in the accounts one could separate the liabilities into long-term and current components as shown in Table 1.5.

The difference between the amount €58,181 of short-term liabilities reported in brackets line [33] and the €56,046 reported below of €2,135 is due to the effects of adjustments 1 and 2 above:

Short-term deferred tax liability not reclassified	1,281
Short-term prepaid expenses transferred to accrued liabilities	854
	€2,135

Table 1.5 Disaggregation of liabilities

	Total	Long term	Short term
Minority interests	691	677	14
Financial liabilities	40,430	19,955	20,475
Other liabilities	9,249	620	8,629
Accrued liabilities	32,265[5]	18,130	14,135
Other short-term			43,253
trade liabilities	12,848	55	12,793
Accrued liabilities		18,185	
Total	€95,483	€39,437	€56,046

[5] After adjustments 1 to 3.

(€ millions)

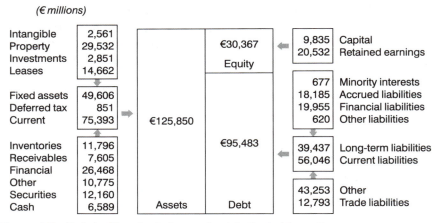

Figure 1.5 DaimlerChrysler balance sheet (adjusted format)

The following calculations reconcile Figures 1.4 and 1.5.

		Liabilities	*Assets*
Amount per Figure 1.4		105,782	136,149
Adjustment 1 Remove			
deferred tax	4,165		
Adjustment 2 Reclassify			
prepaid expenses	6,134		
Adjustment 3 No impact	–	10,299	10,299
Amount per Figure 1.5		€95,483	€125,850

The balance sheet in Figure 1.5 is re-presented in Table 1.6 which now forms a standard format to be the basis of further analysis. This corresponds to the usual Anglo American format and the adjustments 1 to 4 would not be necessary.

There is, however, one major difference between US and UK practices which needs to be identified, that is the display of current liabilities. The US practice is to report on a basis consistent with Table 1.6, however UK companies transfer current liabilities and show them on the asset side of the balance sheet as a deduction from current assets. The different methods have different uses and are illustrated in the context of DaimlerChrysler in summary form below. The total asset approach will be adopted for this section of the book. Figure 1.6 below illustrates the various display options discussed.

The particular display option can have a significant impact on the size of the balance sheet.

It is emphasized that the adjustments we have made are purely related to the display of the various elements which merely involved

Table 1.6 DaimlerChrysler AG Consolidated balance sheets at 31 December. Abridged version

(€ millions)	*1998*
Assets	
Fixed assets	49,606
Deferred tax	851
Current assets	75,393
Inventories	11,796
Trade receivables	7,605
Cash	6,589
Securities	12,160
Other	37,243
Total Assets	€125,850
Liabilities and stockholders' equity	
Stockholders' equity	30,367
Liabilities	95,483
Long-term liabilities	39,437
Minority interest	677
Accured liabilities	18,185
Financial liabilities	19,955
Other	620
Current liabilities	56,046
Financial liabilities	43,253
Trade liabilities	12,793
Total liabilities and stockholders' equity	€125,850

regrouping and reclassifying certain items on the balance sheet. This was made possible with information disclosed in the footnotes to the accounts.

No attempt has been made to adjust any of the amounts reported on the balance sheet for the effects of accounting policies. This means that the resultant balance sheet is based on the original set of accounting policies. A number of these policies were identified during our tour of the balance sheet. All financial statements are issued with a health warning and reading the accounting policy notes which accompany the financial statements is critical. Unfortunately a clean auditor's report merely confirms that management have adhered to the rules when preparing the accounts, there is considerable discretion in choosing accounting policies that can have a significant effect on the numbers. Adjusting for different accounting policies is not covered here and the help of an expert is recommended. We will accept the accounting policies adopted by management as being the most appropriate.

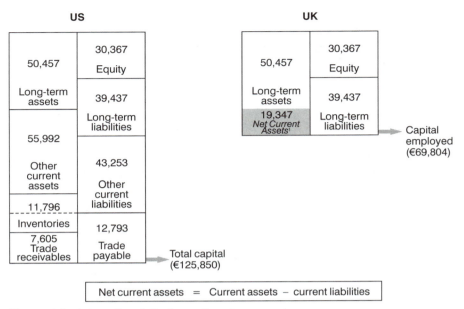

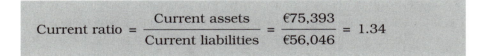

Net current assets = Current assets – current liabilities

Figure 1.6   International display options in use

1.6 What does the balance sheet reveal?

Before moving on to the next section of the financial statements, the new format we have developed for DaimlerChrysler immediately allows us to introduce a few more key ratios.

1.6.1 The current ratio

This is calculated as follows:

$$\text{Current ratio} = \frac{\text{Current assets}}{\text{Current liabilities}} = \frac{€75,393}{€56,046} = 1.34$$

   This tells us that DaimlerChrysler has €1.34 in current assets for every €1 in current liabilities. Therefore if in the unlikely event of having to repay all of its current liabilities overnight it would have 34c per €1 in current liabilities as change or €19,347, the difference between the current assets and current liabilities. This difference is known as net current assets.

   The ratio therefore reveals the short-term solvency of the business, if above 1 the firm is solvent in the short term.

The rough benchmark for industrial companies is a ratio of 2:1. If larger it means that the firm may have an excess of working capital which although solvent may not be a positive sign and may reflect excessive inventory or excess idle cash.

There are of course many types of companies and this benchmark is not universal. Generally companies requiring small inventory and having easily collectible receivables can operate on a lower current ratio.

1.6.2 The quick ratio

This ratio removes the non-liquid inventories number from the current ratio. This ratio measures if the firm would be able to repay its short-term liability assuming inventory is not sold. This ratio requires a calculation of the quick assets of the business.

Current assets	75,393
Less: inventories	11,796
Quick assets	€63,597

The quick ratio is calculated as follows:

$$\text{Quick ratio} = \frac{\text{Quick assets}}{\text{Current liabilities}} = \frac{€63,597}{€56,046} = 1.13$$

This means that DaimlerChrysler's quick assets are enough to cover current liabilities, at 1.13 this is just above the usual benchmark of 1.

1.6.3 Net working capital

Thus far we have introduced two terms that do not appear on the face of the balance sheet but require a separate calculation.

1.	*Net current assets*	
	Current assets	75,393
	Less: current liabilities	56,046
	Net current assets	€19,347
2.	*Quick assets*	
	Current assets	75,393
	Less: inventories	11,796
	Quick assets	€63,597

A third which we will use is net working capital

3. *Net working capital*

Inventories	11,796
Receivables	34,073
Trade receivables	7,605
Financial receivables	26,468
Working capital	45,869
Less: Trade payables	12,793
Net working capital	€33,076

This will be the measure we use to investigate the flow of cash through the business.

1.6.4 Leverage, debt equity and debt ratios

Three balance sheet ratios that describe how the firm is financed are useful. The debt ratio was defined and calculated earlier:

$$\text{Debt ratio} = \frac{\text{Total liabilities}}{\text{Total assets}} = \frac{€95,483}{€125,850} = 75.87\%$$

This tells us that 75.87% of DaimlerChrysler's assets are debt financed. Notice that this ratio is slightly less than the 77.7% we calculated on the unadjusted balance sheet.

The debt to equity ratio is often used to measure how the firm is financed. This is calculated as follows:

$$\text{Debt–equity ratio} = \frac{\text{Total liabilities}}{\text{Equity}} = \frac{€95,483}{€30,367} = 3.14$$

This reveals that DaimlerChrysler has €3.14 in debt for every €1 in equity. Finally, another measure we will use is the leverage ratio. This is calculated as follows:

$$\text{Leverage} = \frac{\text{Total assets}}{\text{Equity}} = \frac{€125,850}{€30,367} = 4.14$$

This ratio reveals that €4.14 are working in assets for every €1 in shareholders' equity; this shows the extent of the leverage that equity has on the use of debt. Notice that Leverage is equal to Debt Equity plus 1.

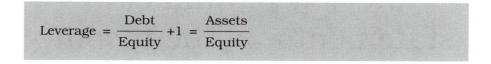

$$\text{Leverage} = \frac{\text{Debt}}{\text{Equity}} + 1 = \frac{\text{Assets}}{\text{Equity}}$$

1.7 What is missing from the balance sheet?

In addition to the various intangibles that were discussed earlier, there are a number of other off-balance sheet financial items that warrant mentioning.

Contingent liabilities are potential liabilities that although material are not certain to be realized. Since management are able to reasonably estimate the amount involved they are reported off balance sheet as a footnote. DaimlerChrysler reported €3,359 of contingent liabilities chiefly relating to guarantees they had made on behalf of affiliated companies. DaimlerChrysler also reported a number of class action claims pending agreement and although material, management were unable to reasonably estimate the amounts, therefore no amount was reported.

In June 1998 The Financial Accounting Standard Board, the American authority on accounting standards issued a statement entitled 'Accounting for Derivative Instruments and Hedging Activities' (SFAS 133). This standard will require companies to record on balance sheet derivatives as assets and liabilities at fair value. Gains or losses assessed on changes in fair value will typically have to be recognized. Currently DaimlerChrysler and most other non-US companies have yet to adopt such a practice, therefore transactions involving derivatives are recorded only after they mature and are realized in cash flow. This means that large exposures to risk are not revealed. The new statement is most welcome and it is expected that leading companies around the world will adopt this as best practice in the future.

The next chapter introduces the income statement and statements of cash flow.

Review of financial statements 2: The income statement and the statement of cash flows

2.1 Introduction to flow statements

This chapter introduces the income statement and cash flow statement. These statements are flow statements which measure the flow of transactions over a period of time as distinct from the balance sheet which reports stocks at a particular moment.

2.2 The income statement

The consolidated statements of income for DaimlerChrysler is reproduced in Exhibit 2.1. This reports an even more daunting array of numbers than the balance sheet, here we see seven separate statements of income reported.

As with the balance sheet the first two columns from the left report the line item headings and references to footnotes, representing the next four columns are the consolidated income statements for the group (columns 3–6), the first reports the current year (1998) in $ terms the next three report the income statement in Euros for the current year and the previous two years. The last three columns (7–9) report the income statements for the financial services sector of the group for the last three years in Euros.

It is common practice to report two years of balance sheet data and three years of data for income statements and cash flow statements. As with our analysis of the balance sheet we will focus on the most recent year in € terms.

Exhibit 2.1 DaimlerChrysler income statement (annotated)

	Note	1998 (Note 1) $	Consolidated Year ended December 31, 1998 €	1997 €	1996 €	Financial Services Year ended December 31, 1998 €	1997 €	1996 €

CONSOLIDATED STATEMENTS OF INCOME

(in millions, except per share amounts)

		Note	1998 (Note 1) $	1998 €	1997 €	1996 €	1998 €	1997 €	1996 €
1	Revenues	30	154,615	131,782	117,572	101,415	7,908	6,545	5,548
2	Cost of sales	5	(121,692)	(103,721)	(92,953)	(78,995)	(6,157)	(5,075)	(4,347)
3	Gross margin		32,923	28,061	24,619	22,420	1,751	1,470	1,201
4	Selling, administrative and other expenses	5	(19,041)	(16,229)	(15,621)	(13,902)	(921)	(760)	(652)
5	Research and development		(5,833)	(4,971)	(4,408)	(4,081)	-	-	-
6	Other income	6	1,425	1,215	957	848	106	82	58
7	Merger costs	1	(803)	(685)	-	-	-	-	-
8	Income before financial income and income taxes		8,671	7,391	5,547	5,285	936	792	607
9	Financial income, net	7	896	763	633	408	23	4	-
10	Income before income taxes and extraordinary item		9,567	8,154	6,180	5,693	959	796	607
11	Tax benefit relating to a special distribution				1,487[1]				
12	Income taxes				(1,005)[2]				
13	Total income taxes	8	(3,607)	(3,075)	482	(1,547)	(361)	(307)	(234)
14	Minority interest		(153)	(130)	(115)	23	(2)	(1)	(2)
15	Income before extraordinary item		5,807	4,949	6,547	4,169	596	488	371
16	Extraordinary item: loss on early extinguishment of debt, net of taxes	9	(151)	(129)	-	(147)	-	-	-
17	Net income		5,656	4,820	6,547[2]	4,022	596	488	371
	Earnings per share	31							
	Basic earnings per share								
	Income before extraordinary item		6.05	5.16	6.90	4.24	-	-	-
	Extraordinary item		(0.16)	(0.13)	-	(0.15)	-	-	-
	Net income		5.89	5.03	6.90[2]	4.09	-	-	-
	Diluted earnings per share								
	Income before extraordinary item		5.91	5.04	6.78	4.20	-	-	-
	Extraordinary item		(0.16)	(0.13)	-	(0.15)	-	-	-
	Net income		5.75	4.91	6.78[2]	4.05	-	-	-

(Annual Report 1998 p. 68)

In contrast to the balance sheet which provides a financial snapshot of the company at a moment in time, the income statement reports the results of a series of transactions that have occurred over a period. For this reason the caption at the top of the page reproduced in Figure 2.2 states 'year ended December 31' as distinct from the 'At December 31' on the balance sheet. While the balance sheet showed the assets of the group, the solvency and how the assets are financed, the income statement shows how profitable the firm has been over a period.

The essential equation for the income statement is shown in Figure 2.1. The 'twin towers' format is presented to show the various elements in relation to sales.

	Net income 4,820
	Taxes 3,075
	Financial (504)
	Expenses 20,607
€131,782	€103,721
Sales	*Cost of sales*

Figure 2.1   The income statement equation

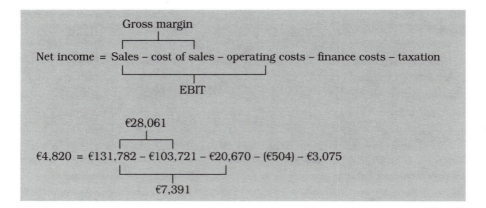

We will now work our way through each item reported on the DaimlerChrysler income statement.

[1]   Revenues   **€131,782**

The revenue number reports the total of sales transactions outside the group. The term revenues, sales and turnover are used inter-changeably. These transactions are the source of most of the money generated by the company. However, these transactions are recorded when the goods and services are delivered to the customer and *not* when customers actually pay. This so-called accrual basis of account-ing gives rise to a difference between income and cash flow so that at the end of the period any outstanding amounts from customers are reflected in sales and held as a current asset (receivables). When the cash is received the cash at bank increases and receivables are reduced; there is no impact on the income statement. The breakdown of sales by type and region is usually reported under segmental information in the annual report. The term net revenues (or sales) is often used to indicate that any discounts are shown as a reduction of sales and not as a separate cost.

After the revenue for the period has been identified, the next step in the determination of income is the matching of cost to the revenues of the year.

[2] Cost of sales	€(103,721)[1]

In a manufacturing operation cost of sales represents all costs incurred in the factory to convert raw material to finished goods. These costs are often referred to as product costs. These are costs identified with the purchase and manufacture of goods available for sale. The costs are often classified as direct materials, direct labour and manufacturing overhead. The direct costs are so called since they are directly traceable to a product; overheads are not directly associated with any particular product. The allocation of these costs across products is an important process to establish the profitability of each product line and it is usually based on a careful analysis of the various activities in the manufacturing process. This problem of allocating costs across product lines is less important in determining aggregate income. However, the allocation of the period manufacturing costs between cost of sales and inventory has a potentially significant impact on the determination of income. This allocation demonstrates well the way in which the determination of income and the determination of the costs of assets are so intrinsically linked. The more of the period costs allocated to inventory the lower the cost of sales. The cost of sales can also include amounts of depreciation where manufacturing overheads are included. This dual determination of cost of sales and inventory is of course based on the principle of matching costs to revenues.

[3] Gross margin	€28,061

Gross margin is the excess of sales and cost of sales. Expressing the gross margin as a percentage of sales is a useful ratio to indicate the extent to which the firm is able to charge a mark-up.

[1] Brackets indicate a change in sign, in this case cost of sales is deducted from sales.

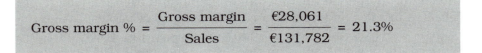

$$\text{Gross margin \%} = \frac{\text{Gross margin}}{\text{Sales}} = \frac{\text{€28,061}}{\text{€131,782}} = 21.3\%$$

Operating costs[2]	€(20,670)

The next four items that appear on the income statement have been added together as operating costs. These are:

[4]	Selling, administrative and other expenses	(16,229)
[5]	Research and development	(4,971)
[6]	Other income	1,215
[7]	Merger costs	(685)
	Operating costs	€(20,670)

[4] Selling, administrative and other expenses	€(16,229)

These numbers include all marketing costs and salaries of marketing personnel; all administration costs and the amortization of goodwill is included as other costs. It is not obligatory to include goodwill amortization in this line. Again these costs are recognized on an accrual basis.

[5] Research and development	€(4,971)

Innovation is an important part of an automaker's competitive advantage so not surprisingly considerable resources are diverted to research and development. While the benefits from the outlays will only appear as revenue in future years the prudence principle overrides the matching principle and the outlays are expensed or recognized in the year spent, as with all costs, on an accrual basis. DaimlerChrysler usually spends around 4% of sales on research and development.

Many companies make the case that when the development is identified with a particular product the costs should not be expensed but accumulated as an asset and finally amortized as a cost against the revenues therefrom, when recognized in income.

[2] Operating costs are not reported separately.

[6] Other income	€1,215

As an inevitable part of operations small amounts of income are earned by the firm. In the case of DaimlerChrysler this includes the profit on the sale of property plant and equipment, subsidiaries and other assets. In addition it earns incidental income in the form of rents and it has enjoyed some foreign exchange gains on its operations.

These are included as a reduction in operating costs rather than as part of revenues.

[7] Merger costs	€(685)

There were some specific costs relating to the merger itself; these are likely to include large amounts of lawyers' and bankers' fees. They are logically treated as part of the cost of operation.

[8] Income before income taxes and extraordinary items	€7,391

This represents the profit remaining after deducting all operating expenses from gross margin. It reflects the profit attributed to operating activities before tax and any financial items. It is a useful number in that it is the only measure of the profitability reported by companies that is not affected by the way a firm is financed. It is usually known as EBIT which is an acronym for Earnings Before Interest and Tax. While it is useful to have a profit measure unaffected by financial items the drawback is that it is before tax. This comes about from the convention relating to the order in which expenses are displayed, taxes always appearing after financial items. Later we will construct a measure not reported by companies called EBIAT, Earnings Before Interest After Tax, which avoids this problem.

[9] Financial income, net	€763

The line item immediately after EBIT reflects the net effect of financial transactions on income. DaimlerChrysler, it turns out, earned more financial income than it paid interest during 1998. The breakdown provided in the notes to the income statement is:

Financial income	1,465
Interest paid	(702)
	€763

Financial income consists mainly of interest and dividends received on investments. Two additional items lower down the income statement are also financial in nature, 'minority interests' and 'loss on early extinguishment of debt' reported as an extraordinary item. Later we will group these items with other financial net income.

[10] Income before income tax and extraordinary items	€8,154

This represents a sub-total on the income statement which is:

[8]	Income before financial income and income taxes	7,391
[9]	Financial income, net	763
[10]	Income before income taxes and extraordinary item	€8,154

[13] Total income taxes	€(3,075)

In section 1.3.3 of Chapter 1 deferred taxes were dealt with in some detail, here we encounter the income statement effects. The total income taxes for DaimlerChrysler consist of two separate elements, one is cash payable on current year income and the other is a non-cash, book-keeping adjustment for deferred taxes:

Current taxes	(1,116)
Deferred taxes (non-cash)	(1,959)
Total income taxes	€(3,075)

It will be noted that the reported effective tax rate reported for DaimlerChrysler is 37.7%. This is calculated as follows:

$$\text{Effective reported tax rate} = \frac{\text{Total income taxes [13]}}{\text{Income before income taxes and extraordinary item [10]}} = \frac{€3,075}{€8,154} = 37.7\%$$

This turns out to be much less than the original German corporate tax rate of 56% (corporate income tax 47,475% plus the after funded tax benefit from trade tax of 8,525%). The difference would have been much greater without the deferred tax adjustments since the actual effective tax rate for the group is only 13.7% based on cash paid. The reason that the deferred tax adjustment does not result in the reported effective tax rate being equal to the marginal corporate rate is that two other factors are at play. First, not all of the group's income is subject to the high German rates, since taxes are determined at the subsidiary level, many of which operate in other countries and tax jurisdictions. Second, there are permanent tax credits available which means that some reported income is shielded from tax permanently.

Line items [11] and [12] relate to an unusual tax benefit relating to the special dividend distribution in 1997 and this was displayed separately. There was no impact in the current year.

[14] Minority interest	€(130)

In section 1.4.2 of Chapter 1 we encountered the item 'minority interests' in the liability segment of the balance sheet. There it was explained how this arose on consolidation and how it was effectively outside financing, provided by minority stockholders in subsidiaries of the group. In a similar way the income statement counterpart represents these minorities' share of the income of such subsidiaries, that are less than wholly owned.

Although not legally debt, but since we have treated the balance sheet items as a liability, it is consistent to treat this expense as a finance cost against the balance sheet amount. This amount is an after tax amount and it does not have the tax effect of interest on debt.

In the rearrangement of the income statement suggested below this item will be re-grouped with the other financial items.

[15] Income before extraordinary items	€4,949

This represents another sub total:

[10]	Income before income taxes and extraordinary items	8,154
[13]	Total income taxes	(3,075)
[14]	Minority interest	(130)
[15]	Income before extraordinary item	€4,949

This represents the famous 'bottom line' in accounting parlance for it is on this number that the primary or basic earnings per share (eps) is calculated and therefore the number that tends to be headlined in the financial press. However, the accounting rules allow extraordinary items to be accounted for below 'the line'.

[16] Extraordinary item	€(129)

In order to be classified below the line as an extraordinary item the transaction giving rise to the income or loss must be outside the ordinary scope of the business. DaimlerChrysler judged that the after-tax losses incurred as a result of the early extinction of debt, was such a transaction. This distinction is becoming less important since the eps is typically reported after extraordinary items as well.

   Since this item is financial in nature we will classify it with the other financial items when we rearrange the income statement.

[17] Net income	€4,820

The final destination on the income statement is the net income. The net income reflects income after absolutely everything. This number also represents the amount by which the shareholders' equity (or the net assets) was increased and is legally available for distribution as a dividend. The income statement thus provides an analysis of the transactions that have affected equity during the year.

   This number provides an input into one of the key financial ratios that measure the profitability of the firm – Net profit (%).

$$\text{Net profit \%} = \frac{[17] \text{ Net income}}{[1] \text{ Revenues}} \quad \frac{\text{€4,820}}{\text{€131,782}} = 3.7\%$$

This means that for every €100 in sales there was €3.70 available for distribution to shareholders. Again, this does not necessarily mean that the firm has the liquidity or the intention to pay out this amount.

2.3 Earnings per share (eps)

For the convenience of investors companies report their income on a per share basis. This allows an easy comparison to the share price which is quoted on a per share basis. Since earnings are based on a full period and if during this period the number of shares in issue has changed, the eps calculation is based on a time weighted average number of shares in issue.

At 31 December 1998 we saw that DaimlerChrysler had 1,001,733,220 ordinary shares in issue. However the weighted average number during the year was 959.3 million.

In the bottom panel of the income statement two types of eps are reported, basic earnings per share and diluted earnings per share. The basic earnings per share is calculated by dividing net income by the weighted average number of shares. The result is in € and not € millions.

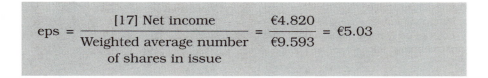

$$\text{eps} = \frac{[17] \text{ Net income}}{\text{Weighted average number of shares in issue}} = \frac{€4.820}{€9.593} = €5.03$$

Under basic earnings per share two other items are shown, based on income before extraordinary items and Extraordinary items.

Base	*eps*
Income before extraordinary items	5.16
Extraordinary item	(0.13)
Net income	5.03

The diluted earnings per share calculates what earnings per share would be if any convertible debt was converted into shares and any other options outstanding were exercised. Net income is adjusted by the interest saving net of tax and the weighted average number of shares is diluted accordingly. The calculations are quite involved but it is usually well reported. The major benefit of disclosing diluted earnings per share is that it provides an indication of the dilutive effects on eps of issuing options either directly or as part of a debt instrument with conversion rights. Clearly as a firm issues new shares there is an immediate dilution effect on eps.

2.4 Rearranging the income statement

Figure 2.1 shows the DaimlerChrysler income statement as 'twin towers'. This analyses revenue into the various elements shown in the income statement equation. The summarized income statement in Table 2.1 shows the rearranged income statement in the conventional format. Notice that operating costs are a grouping of items [4] through

Table 2.1 DaimlerChrysler AG Consolidated statement of income for the year
ending 31 December

(€ millions)	Line item[a]	1998
Revenues	[1]	**131,782**
Cost of sales	[2]	−103,721
Gross margin	[3]	28,061
Operating costs	[4+5+6+7]	−20,670
Earnings before interest and tax (EBIT)	[8]	7,391
Financial costs net	note	504
Financial income	[9]	1,465
Interest expense	[9]	−702
Minority interest	[14]	−130
Loss of early retirement of debt (net of tax)	[16]	−129
Income before tax	[10]	7,895
Taxes	[13]	−3,075
Current taxes	note	−1,116
Deferred taxes	note	−1,959
Net income	[17]	**4,820**

[a]Refer to Exhibit 2.1

[7] and that minority interest [14] and extraordinary items [16] have
been grouped with financial costs.

    This shows the income statement as defined in our equation in
Figure 2.1.

2.5 What does the income statement reveal?

The income statement reveals the profitability of the firm and three
income statement ratios are identified.

$$\text{Gross margin \%} = \frac{\text{Gross margin [3]}}{\text{Sales (Revenues) [1]}} = \frac{€28,061}{€131,782} = 21.4\%$$

$$\text{Net profit \%} = \frac{\text{Net income [17]}}{\text{Sales (Revenues) [1]}} = \frac{€4,820}{€131,782} = 3.7\%$$

A third useful income statement ratio that we will encounter in the
next chapter is the interest coverage ratio.

Interest coverage (times interest earned)	$\dfrac{\text{EBIT [8]}}{\text{Interest paid}}$	$= \dfrac{€7{,}391}{€702} = 10.5\text{x}$

This ratio tells us how many times interest was covered by operating income before tax. One of the consequences of an increasing reliance on debt is that the interest charge increases and this reduces the margin of safety of the firm has to cover these. This is reflected in a reducing interest coverage. When the coverage reduces to the range 1 to 2 there may be cause for concern.

2.6 The cash flow statement

The consolidated statements of cash flow for DaimlerChrysler are presented in Exhibit 2.2. The statement of cash flow is similar to the income statement in that it reports the results of transactions over a period, this being a statement of flows. The layout as a seven-statement report, is identical to the income statement and we will focus on the 1998 consolidated statement in Euros.

The cash flow statement reports and analyses transactions that have affected the cash account of the firm during the period under review. It is of critical importance for valuations which focus directly on the future cash flows of the business. An additional advantage of the cash flow statement is that it largely avoids the effects of discretionary accounting policies, this makes it more comparable across companies and can sometimes be more useful than the income statement.

The cash flow statement analyses all transactions that go through the firm's bank account and classifies them into three categories.

1 Operational cash flows
2 Investment cash flows
3 Financial cash flows

No attempt is made at assessing profitability which was the purpose of the income statement.

The cash flow statement reported by DaimlerChrysler has a large number of line items that may at first obscure the information contained therein. Notice that there is no footnote column. Thus before the guided tour let us extract the essence of what is reported by examining the accounting identity (equation) that defines the cash flow statement.

Exhibit 2.2   DaimlerChrysler cash flow statement (annotated)

CONSOLIDATED STATEMENTS OF CASH FLOWS

			Consolidated Year ended December 31,			Financial Services Year ended December 31,	
	1998 (Note 1) $	1998 €	1997 €	1996 €	1998 €	1997 €	1996 €
1 Net income	5,656	4,820	6,547	4,022	596	488	371
2 Income (loss) applicable to minority interests	153	130	115	(22)	2	1	2
3 Adjustments to reconcile net income to net cash provided by operating activities:							
4 Tax benefit relating to a special distribution	–	–	(1,487)	–	–	–	–
5 Gain on disposals of businesses	(347)	(296)	(569)	(182)	–	–	7
6 Depreciation and amortization of equipment on operating leases	2,314	1,972	1,456	1,159	1,784	1,429	1,215
7 Depreciation and amortization of fixed assets	6,287	5,359	4,847	4,233	38	27	23
8 Change in deferred taxes	2,298	1,959	(706)	112	399	288	83
9 Extraordinary item: loss on early extinguishment of debt	151	129	–	147	–	–	–
10 Change in financial instruments	(224)	(191)	146	200	–	–	2
11 (Gain) loss on disposal of fixed assets/securities	(432)	(368)	(204)	(65)	(51)	13	–
12 Change in trading securities	294	251	(387)	(171)	–	–	–
13 Change in accrued liabilities	1,665	1,419	840	1,416	44	3	21
14 Change in current assets and liabilities:							
15 – inventories, net	(1,145)	(976)	(744)	(427)	64	(140)	(49)
16 – trade receivables	(807)	(688)	(555)	53	124	23	4
17 – trade liabilities	2,144	1,827	1,709	231	159	1	(30)
18 – other assets and liabilities	1,564	1,334	1,329	(750)	1,107	1,187	(369)
19 **Cash provided by operating activities**	19,571	16,681	12,337	9,956	4,266	3,320	1,280
20 Purchases of fixed assets:							
21 – Increase in equipment on operating leases	(9,733)	(8,296)	(5,914)	(4,045)	(7,238)	(4,889)	(3,458)
22 – Purchases of property, plant and equipment	(9,568)	(8,155)	(8,061)	(6,721)	(37)	(24)	(12)
23 – Purchases of other fixed assets	(358)	(305)	(264)	(215)	(60)	(38)	(13)
24 Proceeds from disposals of equipment on operating leases	3,466	2,954	2,632	1,730	2,270	1,905	1,794
25 Proceeds from disposals of fixed assets	604	515	576	660	15	21	6
26 Payments for acquisitions of businesses	(1,006)	(857)	(607)	(236)	(43)	(64)	(83)
27 Proceeds from disposals of businesses	804	685	1,336	1,105	3	–	283
28 Additions to receivables from financial services	(95,264)	(81,196)	(70,154)	(56,880)	(81,259)	(71,221)	(58,126)
29 Repayments of receivables from financial services:							
30 – Finance receivables collected	39,638	33,784	22,257	15,892	33,784	23,114	17,042
31 – Proceeds from sales of finance receivables	48,046	40,950	44,336	39,474	40,950	44,336	39,474
32 Acquisitions of securities (other than trading)	(5,418)	(4,617)	(5,190)	(4,024)	(2,602)	(1,701)	(1,475)
33 Proceeds from sales of securities (other than trading)	3,208	2,734	3,828	4,649	2,487	1,763	2,382
34 Change in other cash	(1,926)	(1,641)	685	(134)	(187)	(739)	(656)
35 **Cash used for investing activities**	(27,507)	(23,445)	(14,530)	(8,745)	(11,917)	(7,537)	(2,842)
36 Change in commercial paper borrowings and short-term financial liabilities	2,937	2,503	1,781	2,828	3,639	1,679	1,389
37 Additions to long-term financial liabilities	11,135	9,491	9,057	2,440	9,169	7,037	3,174
38 Repayment of financial liabilities	(4,841)	(4,126)	(4,612)	(5,228)	(5,073)	(3,844)	(3,035)
39 Dividends paid (Financial Services: incl. profit transferred from subsidiaries)	(7,572)	(6,454)	(1,267)	(746)	(589)	(491)	(479)
40 Proceeds from issuance of capital stock	4,782	4,076	231	231	515	176	248
41 Purchase of treasury stock	(198)	(169)	(1,888)	(1,570)	–	–	–
42 Proceeds from special distribution tax refund	1,744	1,487	–	–	–	–	–
43 **Cash provided by (used for) financing activities**	7,987	6,808	3,302	(2,045)	7,661	4,557	1,297
44 Effect of foreign exchange rate changes on cash and cash equivalents up to 3 months	(466)	(397)	646	351	(28)	36	24
45 Net increase (decrease) in cash and cash equivalents up to 3 months	(415)	(353)	1,755	(483)	(18)	376	(241)
46 Cash and cash equivalents (up to 3 months): at beginning of period	7,783	6,634	4,879	5,362	699	323	564
47 at end of period	7,368	6,281	6,634	4,879	681	699	323

(Annual Report 1998 p. 70)

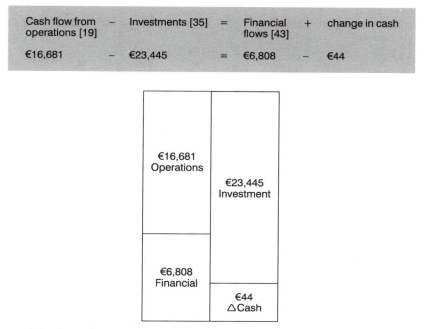

Figure 2.2   Cash flows

This may be better understood if displayed visually. Figure 2.2 reports that DaimlerChrysler's cash flow statement as a 'twin towers' diagram which reflects the equation.

On the left we report the cash inflows and on the right the cash outflows. Here it is immediately clear that investment of €23,445 far exceeded the cash flow from operations of €16,681 which therefore required a net inflow from outside financing of €6,764.

[19]	Cash from operations	16,681
[35]	Less: Investments	(23,445)
	Minimum new funding required	(6,764)
[43]	Actual new funding	6,808
[44+45]	Net increase in cash	€(44)

It turns out that DaimlerChrysler acquired new funding of €6,808, the excess of €44 went to increase the cash at the bank. Figure 2.3 further analyses the key items reported on the cash flow statement of DaimlerChrysler. It will be generally understood that once you have managed to extract the key equation above, the other items are merely providing further information which allows you to have a deeper insight into the cash transactions but also to make explicit the articulation between the income statement and cash flow statement.

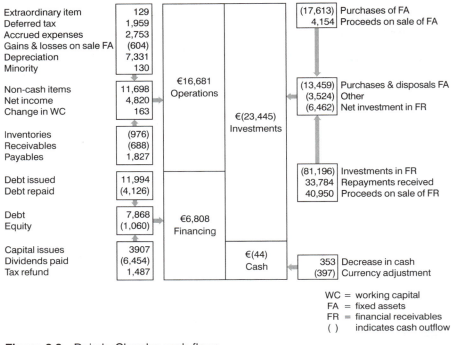

Figure 2.3   DaimlerChrysler cash flows

2.6.1 Operational cash flows

| [19]   Cash provided by operating activities | €16,681 |

The statement begins with net income of €4,820 [1] which was the last line of the income statement and goes on to reconcile this amount in some detail to the cash from operations number. These items are summarized as follows:

[1]	Net income	4,820
	Non-cash items	11,698
	Change in working capital	163
	Cash from operations	€16,681

| Non-cash items | €11,698 |

This amount is made up of the following items reported on the cash flow statement.

[2]	Income applicable to minority interest		130
[5]	Gain on disposal of business	(296)	
[10]	Change in financial instruments	(191)	
[11]	Gain on disposal of fixed asset/ securities	(368)	
[12]	Change in trading securities	251	
	Gains on assets		(604)
[6]	Depreciation and amortization of equipment on operating leases	€1,972	
[7]	Depreciation and amortization of fixed assets	5,359	
	Depreciation		7,331
[8]	Change in deferred taxes		1,959
[9]	Extraordinary item		129
[13]	Change in accrued liabilities	1,419	
[18]	Change in other assets and liabilities	1,334	
	Accruals		2,753
	Non-cash items		€11,698

All of these items were included in net income, however, since they did not involve any cash transactions they are removed. This reflects an indirect method of establishing the net effect of those operational transactions that do affect cash. A more tedious alternative for companies would be to review all cash transactions and report those that were operational.

It is quite usual for depreciation to be the most significant non-cash item. This along with deferred tax and goodwill amortization means that the firm's accounting policies with respect to these items do not affect cash flow. Notice that minority interest and the extraordinary item also did not involve cash flows and so are removed. Since income is derived on the basis of accrual accounting all such amounts not involving cash are removed as well.

Finally gains and losses on fixed assets which although involving cash flows are not operational but form part of investment flows. These are included in the accounts as proceeds or disposal of assets reported in the investment section below.

Change in net working capital	€163

The last element in the reconciliation of net income and cash flow is the adjustment for changes in net working capital, in this case the adjustment increases cash flow and it represents a decrease in net working capital. The amount is made up as follows:

[15]	Inventories, net	(976)
[16]	Trade receivables	(688)
[17]	Trade liabilities	1,827
		€163

Since we saw that revenues and costs in the income statements are recognized when goods and services are invoiced there is a lag between a transaction being recognized in the income statement and it passing through the bank as cash.

Transactions that are incomplete in this way cause a difference to arise between net income and cash flows. The amounts outstanding at the beginning of the year in trade receivables and payables affect cash only and the items at the end of the year affect income only. Therefore the difference between the opening and closing balances on trade receivables and payables has to be reversed out of net income to calculate actual cash flows.

The amounts reported in the cash flow statements represent that part of the change in both receivables and liabilities that affect income. Other transactions affect these items that do not have impact income such as in the sale or purchase of a subsidiary and so no adjustment is necessary.

	Trade receivables	Trade payables
Closing balance per balance sheet	7,605	12,848
Opening balance per balance sheet	7,265	12,025
Change	340	(823)
Recognized in income	(688)	1,827
Net effect on income	€(348)	€1,004

The change in Inventories does however impact cash. Assume a firm purchased all goods for cash, this amount would be apportioned between cost of sales (income statement) and inventory (balance sheet), therefore income is overstated relative to cash flow. However this amount is carried forward and income is then understated as inventory is included in cost of sales when inventory is sold, therefore the change in inventory is reversed out of income to calculate cash flow.

This difference between inventory and the other items of working capital is rather subtle but takes on an importance later.

In summary the adjustment for receivables and payables is simply because they represent non-cash transactions included in income.

Inventory on the other hand is brought to account because it is a cash flow item *not* included in income being reclassified as an operational flow instead of an investment flow. Most companies report on the same basis as DaimlerChrysler.

The 'Cash provided by operating activities' reported by Daimler-Chrysler has the following features.

1 It is a cash flow amount
2 It is after tax
3 It is after finance costs
4 It is after investment in net working capital

The latter two features will need some further attention in order to develop a measure for valuation.

2.6.2 Investment cash flows

[35] Cash used for investing activities	€(23,445)

This amount is analysed into three categories as follows:

Net purchases of fixed assets		€(13,459)
Purchases	(17,613)	
Disposals	4,154	
Net changes in financial receivables		(6,462)
Other investment flows		(3,524)
Investment cash flows		€(23,445)

Net purchases of fixed assets	€(13,459)

[20]	Purchase of fixed assets		(16,756)
[21]	Increase in equipment on operating losses	(8,296)	
[22]	Purchase of property, plant and equipment	(8,155)	
[23]	Purchase of other fixed assets	(305)	
[24]	Proceeds from disposals of equipment on operating losses		2,954
[25]	Proceeds from disposals of fixed assets		515
[26]	Payment for acquisition of business		(857)
[27]	Proceeds from disposal of business		685
	Net purchases of fixed assets		€(13,459)

It may be more helpful to lay out the data in the format shown in Table 2.2.

Many firms report the totals on the face of the cash flow statement and the further detail in a separate note.

This tabular format shows that during the year DaimlerChrysler bought and sold assets individually and as businesses.

Table 2.2 Analysis of fixed asset purchases

Fixed asset	Purchases	Proceeds	Net
1. Equipment on operating leases	(8,296)	2,954	(5,342)
2. Property plant and equipment	(8,155)	515	(7,640)
3. Other	(305)	–	(305)
4. Business (Acquisitions)/disposals	(857)	685	(172)
Total	€(17,613)	€4,154	€(13,459)

Net changes in financial receivables	€(6,462)

In contrast to the treatment of trade receivables DaimlerChrysler classifies changes in financial receivables as investment flows. It will be argued later that changes in trade receivables and payables could be treated in the same way.

This amount is made up of the following line items from the cash flow statement.

[28]	Additions to receivables from financial services		(81,196)
[29]	Repayments of receivables from financial services		74,734
[30]	Financial receivables collected	33,784	
[31]	Proceeds from sales of finance receivables	40,950	
	Net changes in financial receivables		€(6,462)

This tells us that the firm invested €6,462 more than it received back from financial receivables. However, it seems that most of the proceeds are from selling on finance receivables.

Other investment flows	€(3,524)

Other investment flows reported relate to other financial investments made up as follows:

[32]	Acquisition of securities (other than trading)	(4,617)
[33]	Proceeds from sales of securities	
	(other than trading)	2,734
	Net acquisitions of securities	(1,883)
[34]	Change in other cash	(1,641)
		€(3,524)

Although there is evidently some turnover in securities other than trading, these investments are not classified as operational. The securities are intended for holding in the long term and from time to time there will be some buying and selling.

The change in other cash represents an increase in other cash held by the group – which is logically considered to be an investment. There is a case for classifying *all* cash increases (decreases) as investments (divestments).

2.6.3 Financing cash flows

[43] Cash provided by (used for) financing activities	€6,808

This represents the total flow of cash between the firm and its borrowers and lenders during the year excluding interest payments.

It is useful to categorize these between debt and equity:

	Net flows from the debt markets	7,686
[36]	Change in commercial paper borrowing and	
	short-term financial liabilities	2,503
[37]	Additions to long-term financial liabilities	9,491
[38]	Repayment of financial liabilities	(4,126)
	Net flows to the equity markets	(1,060)
[40]	Proceeds from issuance of capital stock	4,076
[41]	Purchase of treasury stock	(169)
[42]	Proceeds from special distribution tax refund	1,487
[43]	Cash provided by financing activities	€6,808

This section of the cash flow statement reveals that DaimlerChrysler has had to raise additional capital to fund its deficit between cash flow from operations and investments.

It is shown that in addition to this deficit there was an additional net outflow to shareholders of €1,060 which required funding. This was all provided by raising additional debt finance.

[36] Change in commercial paper borrowings and short-term financial liabilities	€2,503

This reflects that DaimlerChrysler issued short-term debt certificates and borrowed more from banks in short-term debt thus increasing cash inflows.

[37] Additional long-term financial liabilities	€9,491

DaimlerChrysler issued new long-term debt for this amount which was a cash inflow.

[38] Repayments of financial liabilities	€(4,612)

This was old debt refinanced during the year and is an outflow of cash.

We will see that this net increase in debt of course increases the financial leverage of the firm which will have both financial advantages and disadvantages.

[40] Proceeds from issuance of capital stock	€4,076

This tells us that DaimlerChrysler raised this amount of additional cash flow by issuing more shares.

[41] Purchase of treasury stock	€(169)

A small amount of cash was used to buy back DaimlerChrysler's own stock.

[39] Dividends paid	€(6,454)

The most significant cash outflow to the equity markets was the payment of a dividend to shareholders. It will be noticed that this amount exceeds current income. This implies that the dividend caused a reduction in retained earnings during the year since they were partly provided for from reserves. This is a purely legal matter since, as mentioned earlier, the retained earnings are not kept in a separate cash account for distribution.

[42] Proceeds from special distribution tax refund	€1,487

This amount represents a special tax refund (deduction) triggered by the payment of the special dividend. It will be noted that this amount was accrued as a reduction of tax expense on the 1997 income statement and held as an accrued liability in the 1997 balance sheet. Therefore in the 1997 cash flow statement it is recorded as a non-cash adjustment to calculate cash flow. Since it has a cash flow effect in the 1998 year it has to be accounted for – classifying it as an equity flow makes the most sense since it was entirely linked to the dividend distribution. Thus the cost of the dividend in cash flow to the firm was only €3,967.

Net increase in cash	€(44)

This represents the surplus of finance raised and finance required and is reflected in an increased cash balance which is similar to an investment in cash. It is made up as follows:

[45] Decrease in cash and cash equivalents up to 3 months	353
[44] Effect of foreign exchange rate changes on cash and cash equivalents up to 3 months	(397)
Net increase in cash	€(44)

[45] Decrease in cash balance	€353

This is a potentially confusing layout in the DaimlerChrysler cash flow statement since if one refers to the balance sheet it will be noted that the change in cash balance is actually €220.

Opening cash per balance sheet	6,809
Closing cash per balance sheet	6,589
Decrease in cash	220
Difference (change in cash equivalent longer than 3 months)	133
Decrease in cash and cash equivalents up to 3 months	€353

The difference is equal to the change in the cash equivalents longer than 3 months. Therefore the cash flow statement analyses changes in cash and cash equivalent of less than 3 months maturity. This is quite unusual and not an obviously helpful way to set out the statement.

The use of a bracket for a decrease in cash on the DaimlerChrylser cash flow statement is confusing since a decrease in cash is equivalent to a disinvestment or an inflow.

[44]	Effect of foreign exchange rates changes on cash and cash equivalents up to 3 months	€(397)

Since the group holds cash balances in many currencies changes in the exchange rate against the (DM) and then the Euro will cause an apparent inflow or outflow of cash in Euro terms.

This arises because the cash balances held in foreign currencies at the start of the period would have been translated into DM (and Euros) at the exchange rate at that date. The same amounts in foreign currencies held at the end of the period are translated at the year end rate of exchange to the DM (Euro). Although no cash has left the group, the amount of cash in DM (and €) terms was reduced. This is shown as a natural part of the analysis of the change in cash balance. Since the amount is an increase in cash it suggests that in aggregate the Dm worked against these currencies in which cash balances were held over the period.

2.7 Rearranging the cash flow statement

The assessment of cash flows lies at the heart of valuing businesses and thus a clear understanding of the various elements of cash flow is critical to an effective understanding of value. Therefore some key elements of the DaimlerChrysler cash flow statements are represented to introduce four important cash flow measures not directly reported by firms, but which are relatively easily derived from the financials.

1 Earnings before interest and after tax (EBIAT)
2 Cash flow from operations after tax (Cfloat)
3 Investment flows
4 Free cash flow

Earnings before interest and after tax (EBIAT)	€5,129

Although not a cash flow measure itself it provides an important link between net income and Cfloat. In addition it represents a useful earnings measure which is independent of the firm's financial structure. This feature enables it to be used as an effective comparison among firms with different financial structures.

EBIAT is an acronym which stands for earnings before interest and after tax. As we saw in the income statement this is not directly reported because the convention is to report interest before tax on the income statement[3]. Thus we use EBIT if an earnings measure before finance costs is required. However, EBIT is before tax and so not an ideal metric of income.

EBIAT is most directly calculated as follows:

[1]	Net income	4820
	Add back: Interest paid net of tax	309
	Interest paid	702
	Less: tax effect @German marginal rate of 56%	(393)
	EBIAT	€5,129

The adjustment above removed the effect of interest on net income, this includes the total interest paid which is reduced by the tax saved *via* the tax deductability of interest. We use the marginal tax rate since the firm has a positive income and each € of this income is taxed at a marginal rate. Even though the company paid tax all over the world it is assumed that interest is incurred at the centre in Germany.

Cash flow from operations after tax (Cfloat)	€16,827

This represents operational cash flow after tax and is therefore the cash flow counterpart to EBIAT. It reflects the cash generated from operations (total assets) before financial costs but after tax. In addition it is before divestment of net working capital. It is calculated from EBIAT.

EBIAT	5,129
Add: Non-cash adjustments	11,698
Cfloat	€16,827

---

[3] An increasingly popular measure among US firms is EBITDA (earnings before interest, tax, depreciation and amortizations). This is a proxy for operational cash flows.

In summary this number is reconciled back to the operational cash flows reported by DaimlerChrysler.

[19]	Cash provided by operating activities	16,681
	Less: Decrease in net working capital	163
		16,518
	Add: Interest paid net of tax	309
	Cfloat	€16,827

In this case the difference is not significant but from here on we will assume Cfloat as the appropriate measure of operational cash flow.

Investment	**€(23,326)**

This is the investment flow adjustment reported by DaimlerChrysler. The first we have met already, the treatment of investment in net working capital as an investment flow. The firm commits large amounts of money to net working capital and although it is continuously converted back to cash the net working capital (NWC) is a permanent feature of most balance sheets.

In the purest terms only the inventory element of NWC is a cash flow item; payables and receivables, which tend to offset one another, are not strictly cash flows and could be ignored. In practice and in this book we will treat all elements of net working capital the same.

The second adjustment is the treatment of the change in cash held as an investment (disinvestment). In the usual treatment the change in cash is the balancing number in the cash flow statement. This reminds us that the cash flow statement is an analysis of the change in cash over the period. Treating this amount as part of investments reminds us that management makes a conscious decision to hold cash balances. This allocation of resources to liquid assets is an investment decision and shareholders rightly expect a return on this capital as well.

The result of this adjustment is a considerably clearer cash flow statement with an explicit balancing of cash flows in and cash flows out.

The amount for investments is easily derived as follows:

[35]	Cash used for investing activities	(23,445)
	Disinvestments in net working capital	163
	Change in cash balance	(44)
	Investments	€(23,326)

Free cash flow (FCF)	€6499

Free cash flow is defined in the equation in Figure 2.4.

Free cash flow reflects the difference between cash generated from operations and cash spent on investment. If the Cfloat exceeds investments the FCF is positive and cash flows out to the providers of capital. If, as in the DaimlerChrysler case, more is spent on investments than was generated in cash from operations the FCF is negative and cash flow is from the providers of capital to fund the deficit.

Free cash flow	=	Cash flow from operations after tax	–	Investment
(FCF)		(Cfloat)		(I)
€6,499	=	€16,827	=	€(23,326)

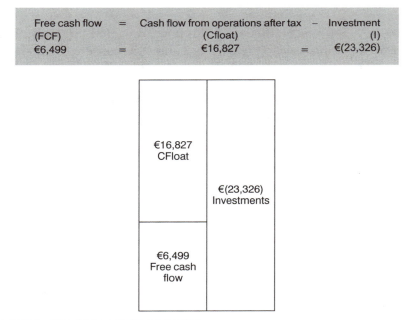

Figure 2.4 The free cash flow equation

The free cash flow therefore represents the net flow of cash between the firm and the providers of the capital.

It is useful to analyse the free cash flows between equity and debt flows to illustrate within each how there are flows in both directions.

Net debt flows	7,559
Net equity flows	(1,060)
Free cash flow	€6,499

In this way, the FCF when analysed have the opposite sign which shows the flows from the firm's point of view. When calculated as Cfloat minus investment the sign indicates the direction of flow from the capital provider's point of view. A negative free cash flow implies a flow of cash into the firm.

The difference in the debt flows is of course the reclassification of interest paid net of tax which was added back to income. It reappears in the analysis of free cash flow as a net outflow to the capital market.

[43]   Cash provided by (used for) financial activities   6,808
         Free cash flow (FCF)   6,499
         Interest paid net of tax   €309

Figure 2.5 analyses further the cash flows reflected in Figure 2.4. In order to be comparable to Figure 2.3. Table 2.3 reorders the cash flows into a standard format. The line items in Table 2.3 are presented to reconcile with the numbers reported by the company in Exhibit 2.2.

This measure of cash flow will be the basis of the central valuation approach taken. The value of the firm being the present value of all future free cash flow.

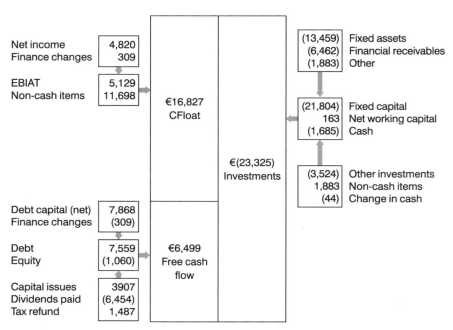

Figure 2.5   Further analysis of cash flows

Table 2.3 DaimlerChrysler AG: Consolidated statement of cash flows for the year ending 31 December

(€ millions)		
Net income		4,820
Interest paid net of tax		309
EBIAT		5,129
Add: Non-cash items		11,698
Cash flow from operations after tax (Cfloat)		**16,827**
Investments		**(23,326)**
Fixed capital		(21,804)
Net working capital		163
Cash		(1,685)
Free cash flow		**€(6,499)**
Analysis of free cash flow		
Debt flows		**7,559**
Capital	7,868	
Interest	(309)	
Equity free cash flows		**(1,060)**
Capital		3,907
Dividend (tax)		(4,967)
Free cash flow		**€6,499**

Although this is correct from a reporting standpoint, in that it is convenient for the users of the financial statement, it would be a mistake to value the business in aggregate. In order to value the business it is necessary to disaggregate these flows to operational flows by business and to isolate the flows from financial assets. Once each business is valued the value of the financial assets would be ascertained separately and added back to the value of the real businesses.

2.8 Summary of financial statement review

This concludes the guided tour of DaimlerChrysler's financial statements and presents a new format as a basis for analysis.

This format converts the rather complex DaimlerChrysler financials into a standard more abridged form which will be basis used throughout the book. In the next chapter we will use this format to analyse the financial health of DaimlerChrysler.

3

Assessing financial health

3.1 Introduction

Financial ratios are the primary tools for the analysis of financial statements which provides the basis for valuing a business and appraising its financial health.

This chapter introduces these concepts in a framework which will be used throughout the book. The financial statements of Daimler-Chrysler, reviewed in Chapters 1 and 2, will form the example for this chapter.

A summary of the ratios dealt with in this chapter is presented in Appendix 3A at the end of the chapter.

3.2 Financial ratios

Tables 3.1 to 3.3 report summary financial statements for Daimler-Chrysler. The income statement and cash flow statements in Tables 3.2 and 3.3 respectively, present data in detail for three years and partially for five. The balance sheet in Table 3.1 is detailed for two years and in summary for five years.

It is usual to base this sort of analysis on five years of data.

Since DaimlerChrysler was only invented recently the annual report reported these data as if the merger had occurred five years ago. However, the detailed data are not available.

It is obvious that a large number of ratios could be calculated for a firm, however, only a few are really meaningful for evaluating financial health. The approach taken here is to focus on a small set of important ratios that identify the critical drivers of value and financial health.

There are four key dimensions to a firm's financial health and the financial ratios will be introduced in these categories.

1 Profitability ratios
2 Efficiency ratios
3 Financial (leverage) ratios
4 Liquidity ratios

Table 3.1 DaimlerChrysler AG: Consolidated balance sheets at 31 December, abridged version

(€ millions)	1998	1997	1996	1995	1994
Assets					
Fixed assets	49,606	44,469			
Deferred tax	851	3,186			
Current assets	75,393	68,244			
Inventories	11,796	10,897			
Trade receivables	7,605	7,265			
Cash	6,589	6,809			
Securities	12,160	10,180			
Other	37,243	33,093			
Total assets	125,850	115,899	101,294	91,597	91,682
Liabilities and stockholders' equity					
Stockholders' equity	30,367	27,960	22,355	19,488	23,316
Liabilities	95,483	87,939	78,939	72,109	68,366
Long-term liabilities	39,437	37,021			
Minority interest	677	782			
Accrued liabilities	18,185	17,145			
Financial liabilities	19,955	18,326			
Other	620	768			
Current liabilities	56,046	50,918			
Financial liabilities	43,253	38,892			
Trade liabilities	12,793	12,026			
Total liabilities and stockholders' equity	125,850	115,899	101,294	91,597	91,682

3.3 How profitable is DaimlerChrysler? – profitability ratios

3.3.1 Profit margin

The profit margin measures how profitable the firm has been with respect to sales.

$$\text{Profit margin} = \frac{\text{Net income}}{\text{Revenues}} = \frac{€4,820}{€131,782} = 3.66\%$$

This shows that for every €100 generated in revenues there remained €3.66 in income.

Table 3.2 DaimlerChrysler AG: Consolidated statement of income for the year ending 31 December

(€ millions)	1998	1997	1996	1995	1994
Revenues	131,782	117,572	101,415	91,040	95,965
Cost of sales	−103,721	−92,953	−78,995		
Gross margin	28,061	24,619	22,420		
Operating costs	−20,670	−19,072	−17,135		
Earnings before interest and tax (EBIT)	7,391	5,547	5,285		
Financial costs net	504	518	284		
Income before tax	7,895	6,065	5,569		
Taxes	−3,075	482	−1,547		
Net income	4,820	6,547	4,022	−1,476	3,499

Table 3.3 DaimlerChrysler AG: Consolidated statement of cash flows for the year ending 31 December

(€ millions)	1998	1997	1996	1995	1994
Net income	4,820	6,547	4,022	−1476	3499
Financial charges net of tax	309	282	256		
Earnings before interest after tax (EBIAT)	5,129	6,829	4,278		
Non cash items included in net income:	11,698	5,380	6,077		
Cash flows from operations after tax (Cfloat)	16,827	12,209	10,355		
Investment cashflows (I)	−23,326	−15,229	−8,054		
Investment in fixed capital	−21,804	−15,215	−8,611		
Investment in net working capital	163	410	−143		
Net investment in cash balances	−1,685	−424	700		
Free cash flows (Cfloat-I)	−6,499	−3,020	2,301		
Analysis of free cash flows					
Net flows with the debt markets	7,559	5,944	−216		
Capital	7,868	6,226	40		
Net financial charges	−309	−282	−256		
Net flows with the equity markets	−1,060	−2,924	−2,085		
Capital	3,907	−1,657	−1,339		
Net dividends	−4,967	−1,267	−746		
Free cash flows	6,499	3,020	−2,301		

The profit margin in 1998 is down from 5.57 in 1997.

DaimlerChrysler	1998	1997	1996	1995	1994
Profit margin	3.66%	5.57%	3.97%	−1.62%	3.65%

It will be noted that the tax expense was very low in 1997 which caused the profit margin to be higher. This reduction in tax was due to an unusual tax refund on a special divided distribution.

The profit margin is based on the bottom line of the income statement and so is affected by all types of costs. It is quite usual to compute different profit measures on the way down the income statement against revenue. This helps to identify major changes in costs.

3.3.2 Gross margin

A usual place to start is gross margin, this reflects the firm's pricing policy and shows profit margin on sales over and above the direct cost of sales.

$$\text{Gross margin} = \frac{\text{Gross margin}}{\text{Revenues}} \quad \frac{€28,061}{€131,782} = 21.29\%$$

This is an increase over the previous year but a reduction against 1996.

DaimlerChrysler	1998	1997	1996	1995	1994
Gross margin	21.29%	20.94%	22.11%	not reported	

3.3.3 Return on assets (ROA)

Investors and managers often are more interested in the profits earned on capital invested than in the level of profits as a percentage of sales. Companies operating in capital-intensive industries often have attractive profit margins but are often less inspiring when the amount of capital absorbed is considered.[1]

Therefore it is useful to examine both the level of and the trend in the company's operating profits as a percentage of total assets. In

[1] Throughout we have taken the closing balance sheet amount in computing ratios. Whenever a balance sheet item is combined with an income statement or cash flow item, the balance sheet item could be averaged between opening and closing amounts.

order to improve the comparisons with other companies, and over time, it is useful to use earnings before interest after tax (EBIAT). This allows one to focus on the profitability of operations without any of the effects of the way in which the assets are financed.

$$\text{Return on assets (ROA)} = \frac{\text{EBIAT}}{\text{Total assets}} = \frac{€5,129}{€125,850} = 4.08\%$$

The trend in ROA has been variable

DaimlerChrysler	1998	1997	1996	1995	1994
ROA	4.08%	5.89%	4.22%	not reported	

3.3.4 Return on investment (ROI)

It is common practice to use net income as the profitability measure against total assets. This is a perfectly legitimate ratio, however, since it is not independent of the way in which the assets are financed a caution is needed when comparing ROIs across firms with very different financial structures.

$$\text{Return on investment (ROI)} = \frac{\text{Net income}}{\text{Total assets}} = \frac{€4,820}{€125,850} = 3.83\%$$

This represented the second best year in the last five on this measure.

DaimlerChrysler	1998	1997	1996	1995	1994
ROI	3.83%	5.65%	3.97%	−1.61%	3.82%

3.3.5 Cash flow return on assets (RonA)

The increasing emphasis on cash flows for valuation has resulted in an improvement in cash flow reporting by firms. This enables analysts to measure returns on assets on a cash flow basis. Thus instead of using EBIAT in the ROA formula, cash flow from operations (Cfloat) is used.

$$\text{Cash flow return on assets (RonA)} = \frac{\text{Cfloat}}{\text{Total assets}} = \frac{€16,827}{€125,850} = 13.37\%$$

Using a cash flow basis the trend in return on asset is quite different.

DaimlerChrysler	1998	1997	1996	1995	1994
RonA	13.37%	10.53%	10.22%	not reported	

3.3.6 Return on equity (ROE)

Finally shareholders are concerned with how profitable the firm is, not per € on the asset base, but per € of stockholders' equity. This is the most commonly used profitability measure and is calculated by taking the net income as a percentage of equity.

$$\text{Return on equity (ROE)} = \frac{\text{Net income}}{\text{Stockholders' equity}} = \frac{€4,820}{€30,367} = 15.87\%$$

This measure shows how hard stockholders funds are working.

For every €100 of stockholders' equity, DaimlerChrysler made €15.87. Is this adequate? 15.87% is certainly better than closing down the business and placing the €30,367 in the bank. However, there are two concerns with this comparison. First, as a stakeholder you will not receive the €15.87 in the €100, you will receive only a smaller dividend return, the rest will be invested and be available in future dividends. Second, this return measure is in book value terms and does not reflect what you would have to pay for your share of the equity. Nevertheless, ROE, probably the most quoted ratio, is shown in Figure 3.1. The trend in ROE is actually the most volatile of any of

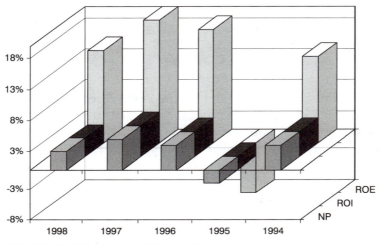

Figure 3.1   Profitability ratios for DaimlerChrysler

Table 3.4   Key purposes of profitability ratios

● Indicate the firm's ability to generate revenues in excess of expenses
● Measure the firm's ability to create value and show how: competitive position is translated to profit margins; efficiency produces cost advantages; profit exceeds capital charges
● Signal the firm's ability to compensate shareholders for risk

---

the other profitability measures. This increased volatility we will see is caused by leverage.

DaimlerChrysler	1998	1997	1996	1995	1994
ROE	15.87%	23.42%	17.99%	−7.57%	15.01%

3.4 How effective is DaimlerChrysler? – efficiency ratios

The efficiency ratios are measures which attempt to evaluate how effectively capital is employed within the firm. The emphasis is on the scale of business generated off the capital base rather than on profitability directly.

3.4.1 Asset turnover

The asset turnover ratio measures how effectively the assets are being worked to generate business as reflected in revenues.

$$\text{Asset turnover} = \frac{\text{Revenues}}{\text{Total assets}} = \frac{€131,782}{€125,850} = 1.045$$

The ratio is usually interpreted as the number of Euros in revenue generated per Euro invested in total assets. Clearly, DaimlerChrysler is a capitally intense business in that each Euro in the asset base generates a €1.05 of revenues. This is to be expected in the auto industry. Utilities are typically even more intense and display asset turnover ratios below 1. In contrast, service organizations generate as much as 6 or 7 Euros per Euro in the asset base.

DaimlerChrysler	1998	1997	1996	1995	1994
Asset turnover	1.05	1.01	1.00	0.99	1.05

Observing the trend in the asset turnover reveals whether the asset base is growing faster than the business. The asset turnover has been relatively constant for DaimlerChrysler which reflects that sales growth rates is similar to asset growth rates.

This ratio is of course affected by the funding of investments. If a new production plant is purchased towards the end of the financial year the balance sheet reflects the full impact in the asset base, however the firm will not yet have enjoyed a full year's revenue from the plant. Thus the ratio will look a little worse when major capital projects are implemented. This ratio represents a common link between two important profitability ratios. The following equation illustrates the importance of asset turnover as a driver of ROI.

$$\frac{\text{Net income}}{\text{Revenues}} \times \frac{\text{Revenues}}{\text{Total assets}} = \frac{\text{Net income}}{\text{Total assets}}$$

$$\frac{€4,820}{€131,782} \times \frac{€131,782}{€125,850} = \frac{€4,820}{€125,850}$$

$$3.66\% \times 1.05 = 3.83\%$$

$$\text{Profit margin} \times \text{Asset turnover} = \text{ROI}$$

It is common to develop asset turnover ratios for different classes of assets included in total assets. The most common are current asset, day's sales in receivables (debtors) and inventory (stock) days.

3.4.2 Day's sales in receivables (DSR)

This ratio compares receivables to sales so as to estimate how efficiently payments are received from customers. The lower the 'day's sales in receivables' the faster cash is collected and the lower the receivables are relative to sales. Thus the overall asset revenue ratio is reduced and ROI increased.

The calculation of this ratio is carried out in two steps.

First, calculate the average revenues per day by dividing revenues by 365.

$$\text{Average revenues per day} = \frac{\text{Revenues}}{365} = \frac{€131,782}{365} = €361$$

Second, divide receivables by average revenue per day. The result is an estimate of the average length of time each customer takes to pay. This reflects the efficiency of managing an important component of working capital.

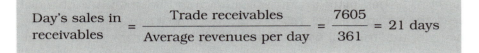

$$\text{Day's sales in receivables} = \frac{\text{Trade receivables}}{\text{Average revenues per day}} = \frac{7605}{361} = 21 \text{ days}$$

The interpretation of this collection period needs to take into account industry practices and should be considered in the context of the overall cash flow cycle[2] and of course the trend over time.

DaimlerChrysler	1998	1997	1996	1995	1994
Day's sales in receivables	21	22.5	not reported		

Cash sales are often deducted from revenues to calculate this ratio. This would obviously increase the average number of day's sales in receivables.

3.4.3 Inventory days

Manufacturers inevitably hold a considerable amount of their capital in the form of inventory. The day's inventory ratio is a useful check on the effectiveness of inventory management. It measures the average number of day's capital tied up in inventory. Inventory days is an important determinant of the firm's cash flow cycle and operates in a similar way to day's sales in receivables.

   Since inventory is held at cost it is necessary to calculate inventory days on the basis of cost of sales.

   The calculation is a two-step process similar to the calculation of the day's sales in receivables.

   First, calculate the average cost of sales per day by dividing cost of sales by 365.

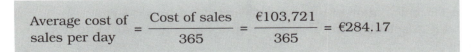

$$\text{Average cost of sales per day} = \frac{\text{Cost of sales}}{365} = \frac{€103,721}{365} = €284.17$$

Second, divide inventory by the average cost of sales per day. The result is an estimate of the average length of time that capital is tied up

[2] See below

in inventory. This reflects management effectiveness in managing working capital.

$$\text{Inventory days} = \frac{\text{Inventories}}{\text{Average cost of sales per day}} = \frac{\text{€}11{,}796}{\text{€}284.17} = 41.51 \text{ days}$$

The shorter the inventory days the lower inventory is in relation to the cost of sales; the asset turnover ratio is reduced (if gross margin is constant or increasing) which in turn will increase ROI.

Inventory days and days in receivables are the important determinants of the firm's cash flow cycle. Observing the trend over time and in comparison to the industry provides some useful insights into the firm's effectiveness of asset management.

DaimlerChrysler	*1998*	*1997*	*1996*	*1995*	*1994*
Inventory days	41.5	42.79		not reported	

The DSR and inventory days ratios will feature again in the liquidity section below.

A summary of the efficiency ratios is given in Table 3.5.

Table 3.5 Key objectives and questions raised by efficiency ratios

---

- Show operational competitive edge
- Indicate the operating efficiency of the firm
- Measure the extent to which the assets are being used to full capacity
- Do the assets sweat?
- Are stock levels too high?
- Are stocks too slow moving?
- Is money collected fast enough?

3.5 How is DaimlerChrysler financed? – financing ratios

The third dimension of financial health is the financial structure of the business. The key ratios indicate the extent of debt financing and how effectively interest is covered.

3.5.1 Debt ratio

This simply indicates the percentage of assets financed by debt.

$$\text{Debt ratio} \quad \frac{\text{Total liabilities}}{\text{Total assets}} = \frac{€95,483}{€125,850} = 76\%$$

There is much variation across industries in this ratio.

DaimlerChrysler	1998	1997	1996	1995	1994
Debt ratio	76%	76%	78%	79%	75%

The debt ratio for DaimlerChrysler has been fairly consistent over the last five years.

Notice that if only interest-bearing liabilities are included the debt ratio drops dramatically.

$$\text{Debt ratio (interest bearing debt)} \quad \frac{\text{Financial liabilities}}{\text{Total assets}} = \frac{39,437 + 43,253}{€125,850} = 66\%$$

3.5.2 Debt equity ratio

Another common way of expressing the debt ratios is by comparing debt to equity

$$\text{Debt equity} = \frac{\text{Debt}}{\text{Equity}} = \frac{€95,483}{€30,367} = 3.14$$

Naturally this will display the same trend over time as the debt ratio.

DaimlerChrysler	1998	1997	1996	1995	1994
Debt equity	3.14	3.15	3.53	3.70	2.93

3.5.3 Leverage ratio

The leverage ratio measures the extent to which shareholders' funds are expanded into productive assets by the use of other funding. This leveraging of shareholders' funds is critical if shareholders seek a return greater than the returned generated by the asset base. Leverage is often a crucial element of business plans and accordingly it is often responsible for financial failure.

While increasing leverage improves returns it does increase the volatility in these returns and hence the risk of failure.

$$\text{Leverage} = \frac{\text{Total assets}}{\text{Equity}} = \frac{€125,850}{€30,367} = 4.14$$

DaimlerChrysler	1998	1997	1996	1995	1994
Debt equity	4.14	4.15	4.53	4.70	3.93

The leverage has been static for the last two years reducing from the peak reached in 1995, but not down to the level of 1994 when leverage was 3.93.

The role of leverage in determining ROE is illustrated in section 3.7.

3.5.4 Interest coverage (times interest earned)

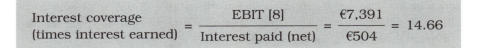

$$\frac{\text{Interest coverage}}{\text{(times interest earned)}} = \frac{\text{EBIT [8]}}{\text{Interest paid (net)}} = \frac{€7,391}{€504} = 14.66$$

This ratio tells us how many times interest was covered by operating income before tax. One of the consequences of an increasing reliance on debt is that the interest charge increases and this reduces the margin of safety the firm has to cover these. This is reflected in a reducing interest coverage. When the coverage reduces to the range 1 to 2 there may be cause for concern.

DaimlerChrysler	1998	1997	1996	1995	1994
Times interest earned	14.66	10.71	18.61	not reported	

As the company has an increasing level of debt it will inevitably have a higher interest charge. However, it appears that EBIT has not kept up with this rate of increase and thus times interest earned was reduced significantly over the last two years. However, interest costs continue to be covered by a considerable margin of safety.

Table 3.6 The key purposes of the financial ratios

- Identify the extent to which non-equity capital is used
- Indicate the firm's long-run ability to meet debt obligations
- Show the financial capacity as a source of competitive advantage
- Measure the margin of safety
- Highlight the extent of financial leverage
- Signal the degree of financial risk

3.6 How liquid is DaimlerChrysler? – liquidity ratios

3.6.1 The current ratio

This is calculated as follows:

$$\text{Current ratio} = \frac{\text{Current assets}}{\text{Current liabilities}} = \frac{€75,393}{€56,046} = 1.35$$

This tells us that DaimlerChrysler has €1.35 in current assets for every €1 in current liabilities. Therefore, if in the unlikely event of having to repay all of its current liabilities overnight DaimlerChrysler would have 35c per €1 in current liabilities as change or €19.347, the difference between the current assets and current liabilities. This difference is known as net current assets.

The ratio therefore reveals the short term solvency of the business, if above 1 the firm is solvent in the short term.

The rough benchmark for industrial companies is a ratio 2:1. If larger it means that the firm may have an excess of working capital which although solvent may not be a positive sign and may reflect excessive inventory or excess idle cash.

There are of course many types of companies and this benchmark is not universal. Generally companies which require small amounts of inventory and have easily collectible receivables can operate on a lower current ratio.

DaimlerChrysler	1998	1997	1996	1995	1994
Current ratio	1.35	1.34		not reported	

The current ratio has been constant for the last two years. This is largely due to the existence of significant cash and cash equivalent balances.

3.6.2 The quick ratio

This removes the non-liquid inventories number from the current ratio. This tests solvency as if the company had to repay all of its current liabilities overnight assuming it would be unable to sell any inventory. This ratio requires a calculation of the quick assets of the business.

Current assets	75,393
Less: Inventories	11,976
Quick assets	€63,597

The quick ratio is calculated as follows:

$$\text{Quick ratio} = \frac{\text{Quick assets}}{\text{Current liabilities}} = \frac{€63,597}{€56,046} = 1.13$$

This means that DaimlerChrysler's quick assets are enough to cover current liabilities, at 1.13 this is just above the usual benchmark of 1.

DaimlerChrysler	*1998*	*1997*	*1996*	*1995*	*1994*
Quick ratio	1.13	1.13		not reported	

The quick ratio remains constant in line with the current ratio which suggests that inventory has grown exactly in proportion to current liabilities.

3.6.3 Payable days – (creditor days)

An important element of a firm's cash flow cycle is the amount of credit it receives from suppliers. The payable day's ratio estimates the average of day's credit taken from suppliers.

Similarly to the day's sales in receivable ratio (see section 3.4.2), the payable days is calculated in two steps.

First, calculate the average purchases per day by dividing purchases by 365. Purchases are estimated as shown in Table 3.7.

$$\text{Average purchases per day} = \frac{\text{Purchases}}{365} = \frac{€104,530}{365} = €286.38$$

Table 3.7   Estimating purchases

Cost of sales		€103,721
Inventory at end of year	€11,796	
Less:		
Inventory at beginning of year	€10,987	
Increase in inventory		€809
Purchases		€104,530

Purchases = Cost of sales + Change in inventory

Second, divide trade payables by the average purchases per day. The result is an estimate of the average length of time the firm takes to pay its trade creditors.

$$\text{Payable days} = \frac{\text{Trade liabilities}}{\text{Average purchases per day}} = \frac{€12,793}{€286.38} = 44.63 \text{ days}$$

The 44.63 days DaimlerChrysler takes to pay reduces the funding requirement for working capital by cushioning the credit extended to customers

DaimlerChrysler	*1998*	*1997*	*1996*	*1995*	*1994*
Payable days	44.63	47.22		not reported	

The 1997 number has been calculated on the assumption that inventory remained constant between 1996 and 1997. This assumption is required as inventory at year end 1996 is not reported.

3.6.4 Cash cycle days

An important aspect of liquidity is the average period of cash in circulation through working capital. The cash cycle in days measures the average elapsed time between an item arriving in inventory being paid for and it finally being realized as cash once the customers pay. The various stages in the cycle are illustrated in Figure 3.2.

    The cash cycle in days is calculated from the three ratios we have encountered.

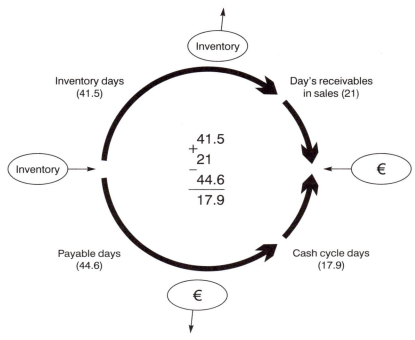

Figure 3.2 Cash flow cycle DaimlerChrysler (1998)

Cash cycle days	=	Inventory days	+	Day's sales in receivables	−	Payable days
17.9	=	41.5	+	21.0	−	44.6

Thus on average cash is tied up in working capital for 18 days. This represents downtime from working capital which will be illustrated as a constraint on short-term growth.

DaimlerChrysler	*1998*	*1997*	*1996*	*1995*	*1994*
Cash cycle (days)	17.9	18.1		not reported	

Table 3.8 The key purposes of liquidity ratios

- Indicate the firm's ability to meet short-term debt obligations
- Show the extent of short-term debt capacity
- Highlight the extent to which finance is provided to/by others
- Identify the working capital constraints on short-term growth
- Draw attention to idle cash

3.6.5 Constraints on short-term growth

All firms regardless of whether they are manufacturers, service businesses or retailers have a flow of cash in and out of the business. This means that all firms have a cash cycle hindering or helping the growth of business. The nature of the business and the competitiveness of the industry will influence the cycle and dictate the options open for management action. Nevertheless, no firm can escape the careful management of this aspect of business life.

The cash cycle days calculated in section 3.6.4 can be demonstrated to provide great insight into the funding requirements of the business in the short term.

Consider the following analysis. DaimlerChrysler is currently experiencing an annual cash cycle of approximately. 18 days. This means that DaimlerChrysler must raise €4.9 in extra working capital for every €100 increase in sales.

$$\text{Additional funding for every €100 income in sales} = \frac{\text{Cash cycle days}}{365} \times 100 = \frac{17.9}{365} \times 100 = €4.90$$

Thus if DaimlerChrysler aims to grow sales by 10% it will enjoy incremental sales of €13,178, however, it will require an investment in working capital of €646.

In the case of DaimlerChrysler this severely underestimates its funding requirement because we have ignored the financial receivables in this calculation. The inclusion of financial receivables increases the day's sales in receivables (section 3.4.2) by increasing receivables from €7,605 (trade) by €26,468 (financial) to €34,073. This increases the day's receivables from 21 days to 94 days. The increase of 73 days immediately increases the cash cycle in days by the same amount to 90.9 days. Recalculating the incremental funding per €100 of extra sales reveals that approximately €25 is now required. Thus a 10% increase in sales of €13,178 will require working capital funding of around €3,294.5 This will absorb a considerable amount of DaimlerChrysler cash balances.

This example illustrates that regardless of profitability the working capital requirements of business can act as a considerable constraint on short-term growth.

As sales grow, capital is typically required to grow as fast to support the business. The cash cycle in days provides a crucial insight into understanding the short-term funding needs of the business. It is emphasized that this funding requirement is not inevitable – managers can and must actively try to reduce the working capital requirement. The cash cycle days is the right measure to focus on when seeking to control and contain the funding requirement of a business.

The cash cycle for many retail businesses is negative, since the goods are sold for cash before they are paid for. Clearly in this case growing the business generates cash flow.

3.7 The drivers of ROE

Figure 3.3 illustrates the critical drivers of return on equity. This format, known as the duPont chart, provides a coherent framework to illustrate the interconnection among three dimensions of financial health.

The chart lays out in the bottom row two items from the income statement (profit and revenues) and two items from the balance sheet (assets and equity).

The next row shows net profit % as the proportion of profit to sales which entirely reflects the profitability of the business. €3.66 was generated in profits for every €100 in sales.

Asset turnover reveals how efficiently the asset base has been worked to generate business as measured by sales. This measure is quite independent of profitability. These two measures combine to create return on investment ROI. Thus ROI is jointly effected by both profitability (net profit %) and by efficiency (asset turnover).

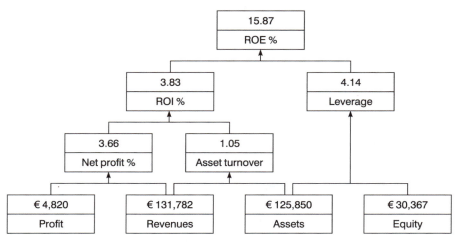

Figure 3.3   The drivers of ROE DaimlerChrysler (1998)

The determinants of ROI are identified below

$$\underbrace{\frac{\text{Profit}}{\text{Revenues}}}_{\text{(net profit \%)}} \times \underbrace{\frac{\text{Revenues}}{\text{Assets}}}_{\text{(Asset turnover)}} = \underbrace{\frac{\text{Profit}}{\text{Assets}}}_{\text{(ROI)}}$$

Finally Figure 3.3 demonstrates the amplification effect of leverage on returns. It illustrates how ROI reflects chiefly the return on the real side of the business[3].

The effect of leverage on returns:

$$\underbrace{\frac{\text{Profit}}{\text{Assets}}}_{\text{(ROI)}} \times \underbrace{\frac{\text{Assets}}{\text{Equity}}}_{\text{(Leverage)}} = \underbrace{\frac{\text{Profit}}{\text{Equity}}}_{\text{(ROE)}}$$

The existence of debt (which increases leverage, gears the ROI to the high return on equity).

Increasing the levels of debt relative to equity has the first-order effect of increasing leverage and therefore ROE.

A central question to be addressed in this book is whether increasing debt increases value. It will be shown that although debt may increase ROE it also increases financial risk which in turn increases the required ROE to compensate. There is additional risk because if ROI is negative leverage works against profitability and ROE is more negative. This is illustrated in Figure 3.4.

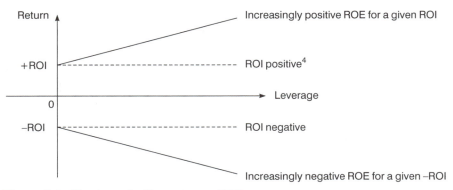

Figure 3.4   The impact of leverage on ROE

[3] Since project is impacted by finance costs, leverage does affect ROI slightly.
[4] Footnote 3 implies a slightly negatively sloping ROI schedule. This effect has been ignored.

It will be demonstrated when we introduce the cost of capital in Chapter 5 that the second-order effect of increasing leverage is an increased risk premium. The impact of increasing leverage on value is not straightforward and involves the consideration of trading off increasing returns with increasing risks, tax considerations and foregone growth opportunities. ROE is an important source of value which is driven by profitability, efficiency and financing.

3.8 Constraints on long-term growth – sustainability

In section 3.6.5 we considered the constraint on short-term growth by observing the cash flow cycle independent of profitability. The mid- to long-term funding requirements of a business are fundamentally driven by the sustainable growth of the business.

3.8.1 The drivers of sustainable growth

Figure 3.5 lays out a chart which illustrates the key determinants of sustainable growth.

The left-hand side of the chart is identical to Figure 3.2, and shows the drivers of ROE. The right-hand side introduces the effect of dividend policy. The ratio of dividends to earnings is known as the payout ratio. This measures the proportion of earnings that have been paid out in the current year. A ratio larger than 1 means that DaimlerChrysler has paid out more dividends than earnings.

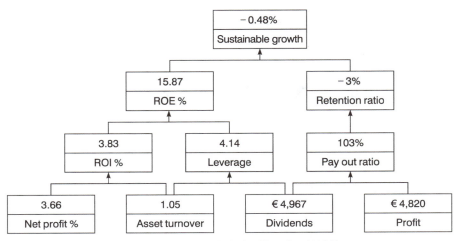

Figure 3.5 Profitability and growth at DaimlerChrysler (1998)

$$\text{Payout ratio (PO)} = \frac{\text{Dividends}}{\text{Earnings}} = \frac{€4,967}{€4,820} = 1.03$$

The retention ratio (rr) is calculated by deducting the payout ratio (po) from 1.

$$\text{Retention ratio (rr)} = (1-po) = (1-1.03) = -0.03$$

Since DaimlerChrysler has paid out slightly more dividends (net of tax) than it had earnings, the retention rate is slightly negative.

Figure 3.5 illustrates that sustainable growth is driven by ROE and rr.

$$\text{Sustainable growth rate (sgr)} = \text{ROE} \times \text{rr} = 15.87\% \times (-0.03)$$
$$= -0.48\%$$

DaimlerChrysler's payout policy illustrates the trade-off between dividends and growth – the larger the payout ratio the lower the retention rate and thus the lower the sustainable growth.

Clearly a business that pays out all of its earnings as dividends will not be able to sustain any growth without resorting to further financing in the form of debt or equity capital.

Figure 3.6 shows the evolution of dividends and earnings over the last three years. Although the 1998 year is unusual due to the

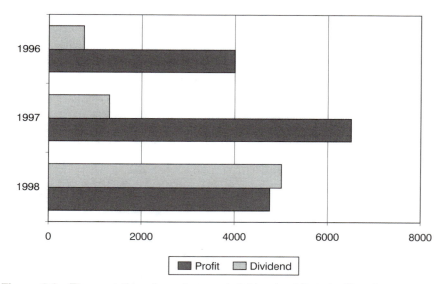

Figure 3.6 The evolution of earnings and dividends at DaimlerChrysler

Table 3.9 Sustainable growth and funding gap

DaimlerChrysler	1998	1997	1996
Net income	4,820	6,547	4,022
Effective dividends	4,967	3,155	2,316
Dividends	4,967	1,267	746
Stock repurchases	–	1,888	1,570
Payout ratio	103.05%	48.19%	57.58%
Retention ratio	−3.05%	51.81%	42.42%
Return on equity (ROE)	15.87%	23.42%	17.99%
Sustainable growth	−0.48%	12.13%	7.63%
Actual growth	12.10%	15.90%	11.40%
Funding gap	−12.58%	−3.77%	−3.77%

payment of a special dividend – it must be pointed out that during years 1997 and 1996 DaimlerChrysler bought back its own stock in the amounts of €1,888 and €1,570 respectively.

Table 3.9 summarizes the behaviour of sustainable growth and actual growth over the last three years for DaimlerChrysler. In this case stock repurchases are included as dividends for the calculation of payout ratio. Stock repurchases have a similar effect to dividends in that they transfer cash from the balance sheet to shareholders. Notice that the differences between actual growth and sustainable growth is described as a funding gap.

Figure 3.7 shows the evolution of the funding gap at DaimlerChrysler.

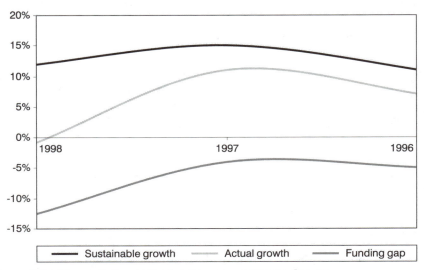

Figure 3.7 The evolution of the funding gap at DaimlerChrysler

3.8.2 How the funding gap arises

In order to deal with the funding gap it is necessary to understand the concept of sustainable growth. The sustainable growth as defined above is not a prediction of the growth a firm will experience nor indeed is it inevitable – however, it represents a bound on the growth a firm can enjoy without adjusting its performance or finding new funding.

If the firm invests its retained earnings in productive assets, increasing debt enough to keep leverage constant, and if the total assets generate sales at the same rate as previously and if profitability rates on sales are similar the income statement and balance sheet will expand at the same rate.

This rate of expansion is the sustainable growth. If a firm attempts to grow above this rate it will experience funding difficulties unless other measures are taken.

If, for example, DaimlerChrysler, seeks to grow at 10% over the next year, revenues will need to be grown from the current level of €131,782 to approximately €144,960, if the asset turnover ratio remains constant total assets will need to grow at the same rate and thus €12,850 of new funding is needed.

This requirement cannot be funded from last year's retained earnings as there are none – therefore leverage must be increased or new equity raised.

The sustainable growth rate times total assets represents that amount of funding that can be sustained by the business without changing its capital structure and without resorting to new equity capital.

Any firm growing above its sustainable growth rate inevitably requires increasing injections of capital equal to the difference between the sustainable and actual rates times the asset base.

> Additional funding = Actual – Sustainable growth ×
> requirement   Total assets growth
>
> = 10% – (–0.48%) × €125,850 = €13,189

DaimlerChrysler therefore requires a little more that 10% of its assets in new funding to grow at 10%, because its sustainable growth is slightly negative.

3.8.3 Dealing with the funding gap

Consider again Figure 3.5. If DaimlerChrysler seeks to grow sales at 10% it has a number of alternatives.

1. Change in dividend policy

If DaimlerChrysler could target to maintain ROE of 15.87% and adjust upwards its retention rate to around 63%, the result would be sustainable growth of around 10%, however, the payout ratio would be reduced to 37% which may disturb shareholders and reduce the stock price.

If DaimlerChrysler was able to increase its retention rate to say 25% and the payout was reduced to 75% the sustainable growth at the current level of ROE would be around 4%.

At a retention rate of 25% a ROE of 40% would be required to sustain growth at 10%.

2. Increase leverage

The easiest way to increase ROE is to increase leverage. In order to achieve a 40% ROE given an ROI of 3.83, leverage needs to be increased to above 10. It is unlikely that this would be achievable.

3. Increase profitability or asset efficiency

If payout was reduced to 75% and leverage increased to 6 times ROI would need to be 6.6% to achieve the ROE of 40% required to sustain growth at 10%.

This expanded Dupont chart provides a useful model for evaluating the way in which the various components of financial performance interact with financial policy variables. Performance and policy variables must be balanced to ensure that the firm is adequately financed.

3.9 Understanding the relationships among profitability, financial policy and growth

The previous section on using the Dupont version of sustainable growth is useful to understand the various trade-offs among performance variables and policy variables. The method is approximate and particularly useful as a 'back of the envelope' calculation.

This section sets out a slightly more refined and general version of the model based on cash flows, which is more accessible for use in spreadsheets.

In order to illustrate the approach consider the financial numbers set out in Table 3.10.

The targets identified are a real example of a company that was brave enough to reveal its own expectations.

Table 3.10   Matching financial and business objectives

Financial policies	
• Target debt to equity (D/E)	67%
• Target dividend payout (PO)	25%
Business objectives	
• Return on assets (RonA) (before tax)	28%
• Asset turn	7%
• Return on sales before tax	4%
Market imperatives	
• Growth in sales (g)	20%
Financial market conditions	
• Interest rate on debt (i)	14.4%
• Marginal tax rate	35%

The important variables are classified into four groups, financial policies, business objectives, market implications and financial conditions.

Figure 3.8 sets out the cash flow implications of these targets per €1,000 in the opening asset base. Are these targets internally consistent? The starting balance sheet has €400 in debt and €600 in equity for each €1,000 in the asset base. This is consistent with the target debt/equity of 67%.

How much cash will be generated from operations?

The pre-tax RonA is expected to be 28% which implies a post-tax return of 18.2% after tax of 35%. Thus Cfloat per €1,000 of assets is €182.

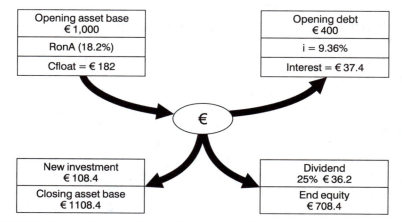

Opening asset base	Opening debt
€ 1,000	€ 400
RonA (18.2%)	i = 9.36%
Cfloat = € 182	Interest = € 37.4

€

New investment	Dividend
€ 108.4	25% € 36.2
Closing asset base	End equity
€ 1108.4	€ 708.4

Figure 3.8   A model of cash flow with no new debt

For every €1,000 asset there is €400 debt on which interest is payable at 14.8%. After tax this interest is 9.36%[5]. This represents an after-tax cash payment of €37.4.

What is the equity cash flow available for distribution?

Cfloat	182
Less: interest paid net of tax	37.4
Equity cash flow	144.6
Dividend at 25%	36.23
Retained equity cash flow	€108.4

What dividends are to be paid?

The dividend will be based on the earnings (equity cash flows) with a payment of 25%. Thus €36.2 is paid in dividend per €1,000 in the asset base.

What is available for reinvestment in the asset base?

The retained equity cash flows of €108.4 are then reinvested in the asset base of €1,000. This represents a growth rate of only 10.8%. Clearly this growth falls well short of the stated target growth rate of 20%. What is missing?

In order to understand why the growth rate falls short, consider the closing debt equity ratio. Debt remains at €400, however, equity has now increased to €708.4 resulting in a D/E of 56.5%. The retention of equity cash flows has reduced the D/E. Therefore to hold D/E at the target level, €67.6 can be borrowed for every €100 of retained earnings. Retained earnings are 108.4 therefore €72.3 of additional debt is introduced. This effect is illustrated in Figure 3.9. There is now €180.70 retained which represents an 18% growth rate – this approximates the firm's target rate.

This diagram reflects the crucial financial identities which affect every firm. These are the laws of physics of finance that cannot be avoided. The general format of the model is set out in Table 3.11[6].

Notice that there are five crucial variables, this means that there are four degrees of freedom, once any four are set the fifth is fixed.

The model is extremely useful to develop an insight into the financial trade-offs and imperatives which managers face.

Growth is often set by strategy; interest rates are usually outside management control; which leaves the two financial policy variables – debt and dividends. These are usually bounded quite tightly

---

[5] The after-tax interest charge is calculated as follows: Interest paid × (1-tax rate).
[6] Notice the first item in the equation is equivalent to a cash flow version of ROE. See proof in Appendix 3B.

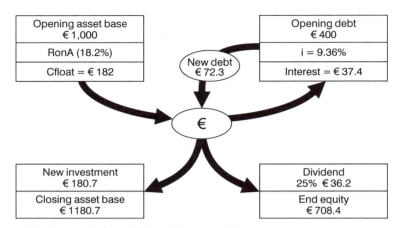

Figure 3.9 A model of cash flow with new debt.

Table 3.11 The consistency test: relating business objectives and financial policies

$$g = \left[RonA + \left(\frac{D}{E} \times \{RonA - i\} \right) \right] \times [1 - PO]$$

$$18\% = [18.2\% + (0.66 \times \{18.2\% - 9.78\%\}) \times [1 - 0.25]$$

where:
g = growth in sales
$RonA$ = return on assets before finance costs
D/E = the proportion of debt to equity
i = the after-tax cost of debt
PO = the proportion of earnings paid out as dividend

by financial markets. This leaves the focus and pressure on operational performance.

3.10 Stock market measures

3.10.1 The price earnings ratio (per)

The most common stock market performance measure is the price earnings ratio. This is calculated by dividing the market capitalization by net income. This is often done on a per share basis.

Crudely this represents the number of years' earnings reflected in the share price. However, this interpretation ignores the growth expected in earnings and the time value of money.

It is emphasized that although the per is used as the way to value companies it is actually a ratio that is determined by the valuation process.

$$\text{per} = \frac{\text{Market capitalization}}{\text{Net income}} = \frac{€83,742}{€4,820} = 17.37$$

DaimlerChrysler traded at a per of 17.37 at 31 December 1998.

3.10.2 Price to book ratio

Another common performance measure is the price to book ratio. This represents the value multipliers applied to the book value of equity by the market. It is computed by dividing market capitalization by stockholders' equity.

$$\text{Price to book} = \frac{\text{Market capitalization}}{\text{Stockholders' equity}} = \frac{€83,742}{€30,367} = 2.76$$

This reflects the fact that DaimlerChrysler have added €2.76 to every € of book equity.

The relationship between the per and price to book ratios is illustrated in Figure 3.10.

The diagram connects the per and P/B with the ROE and illustrates that these metrics are outcomes of the market valuation process rather than inputs.

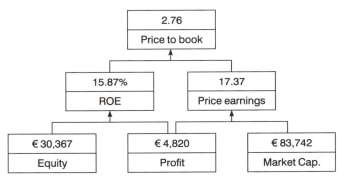

Figure 3.10 The relationship between ROE, per & P/B

3.10.3 Dividend yield

The dividend yield ratio compares dividends to market capitalization.

$$\text{Dividend yield} = \frac{\text{Dividends}}{\text{Market capitalization}} = \frac{\text{€4,967}}{\text{€83,742}} = 5.9\%$$

This concludes the chapter on financial health.

Appendix 3A   Summary of key financial ratios

	Ratio	Formula
A	*Profitability ratios*	
A1	Profit margin	$\dfrac{\text{Net income}}{\text{Revenue}}$
A2	Gross margin	$\dfrac{\text{Gross margin}}{\text{Revenue}}$
A3	Return on assets (ROA)	$\dfrac{\text{EBIAT}}{\text{Total assets}}$
A4	Return on investment	
A5	Cash flow return on asset (RonA)	$\dfrac{\text{Cfloat}}{\text{Total assets}}$
A6	Return on equity	$\dfrac{\text{Net income}}{\text{Total equity}}$
B	*Efficiency ratios*	
B1	Asset turnover	$\dfrac{\text{Revenue}}{\text{Total assets}}$
B2	Days sales in receivables	$\dfrac{\text{Trade receivables}}{\text{Sales}}$
B3	Inventory days	$\dfrac{\text{Inventory}}{\text{Cost of sales}} \times 365$
C	*Financing ratios*	
C1	Debt ratio	$\dfrac{\text{Debt}}{\text{Total assets}}$
C2	Debt equity	$\dfrac{\text{Debt}}{\text{Equity}}$

	Ratio	Formula
C3	Leverage	$$\dfrac{\text{Total assets}}{\text{Equity}}$$
C4	Times interest earned	$$\dfrac{\text{EBIT}}{\text{Interest paid}}$$
D	*Liquidity ratios*	
D1	Current ratio	$$\dfrac{\text{Current assets}}{\text{Current liabilities}}$$
D2	Quick ratio	$$\dfrac{\text{Current assets} - \text{Inventories}}{\text{Current liabilities}}$$
D3	Payable days	$$\dfrac{\text{Trade liabilities}}{\text{Purchases}} \times 365$$
D4	Cash cycle days	Inventory + Receivable days − Payable days

Summary of ratios for DaimlerChrysler	1998	1997	1996	1995	1994
A. **Profitability ratios**					
A1. Net profit	3.66%	5.57%	3.97%	−1.62%	3.65%
A2. Gross margin	21.29%	20.94%	22.11%	−	−
A3. Return on assets (ROA)	4.08%	5.89%	4.22%	−	−
A4. Return on investment (ROI)	3.83%	5.65%	3.97%	−1.61%	3.82%
A5. RonA	13.37%	10.53%	10.22%	−	−
A6. Return on equity (ROE)	15.87%	23.42%	17.99%	−7.57%	15.01%
B. **Efficiency ratios**					
B1. Asset turnover	1.05	1.01	1.00	0.99	1.05
B2. Days sales in receivables (DSR)	21.06	22.55	−	−	−
B3. Inventory days	41.51	42.79	−	−	−
C. **Financing ratios**					
C1. Debt ratio	0.76	0.76	0.78	0.79	0.75
C2. Debt equity	3.14	3.15	3.53	3.70	2.93
C3. Leverage	4.14	4.15	4.53	4.70	3.93
C4. Times interest earned	14.66	10.71	18.61	−	−
D. **Liquidity ratios**					
D1. Current ratio	1.35	1.34	−	−	−
D2. Quick ratio	1.13	1.13	−	−	−
D3. Payable days	44.63	47.22	−	−	−
D4. Cash cycle days	17.94	18.12	−	−	−

Appendix 3B   The relationship between ROE and ROA

ROA is independent of financing and its relationship to ROE is shown in (1)

$$ROE = ROA + (ROA - i)\, D/E \tag{1}$$

Where i is the interest rate after tax payable on debt.
   A proof for (1) is as follows:

   Given the two key identities (2) and (3)

$$Assets = Debt + Equity \tag{2}$$

$$Income = EBIAT - Interest\ net\ of\ tax \tag{3}$$

It is noted that Interest net of tax is iD thus (3) may be re-written as

$$Income = EBIAT - iD \tag{4}$$

Divide (4) by Assets (A)

$$\frac{Income}{Assets} = \frac{EBIAT}{Assets} - i\frac{D}{A} \tag{5}$$

These ratios have been defined as

$$ROI = ROA - i\frac{D}{A} \tag{6}$$

Recall that ROI times leverage (A/E) is equal to ROE.
   Multiply (6) by A/E

$$ROE = ROA\frac{A}{E} - i\frac{D}{A} \times \frac{A}{E} \tag{7}$$

From (2) A/E = D/E + 1.
   By replacement

$$ROE = -ROA\ (D/E + 1) - i\, D/E \tag{8}$$

Rearranging

$$ROE = ROA + (ROA - i)\, D/E \tag{9}$$

The result can be derived directly by intuition.

The ROI of a firm can be thought of as being the weighted average of the return on two hypothetical classes of assets with identical ROAs. The first is 100% equity financed and the second is 100% debt financed. The equity financed assets have no interest burden which is borne completely by the debt-financed assets.

Thus ROI can be written as

$$\text{ROI} = \frac{E}{A} \text{ROA} + \frac{D}{A} (\text{ROA} - i)$$

This illustrates the weighting of returns from the the two assets. Multiply by leverage to derive ROE and the result is equation (1) above where

$$\text{ROE} = \text{ROA} + (\text{ROA} - i)\, D/E$$

Part 2

Valuation

4

The cost of capital: concept and measurement

One of the fundamental parameters of finance is the cost of the financial resources employed by the firm. Money is probably the only common 'raw material' used by any business in any industry. Understanding and assessing the cost of this commodity is essential to all managers, whatever their area of responsibility, which are all regularly spending money. From a management point of view, cost of capital is just another resource cost, it is to capital what wages are to labour. From the investor's perspective, it compensates them for the opportunity cost of time and risk, what they could get elsewhere from comparable investments.

4.1 Thinking about risk and return: a quick overview of capital asset pricing model (CAPM)

4.1.1 Defining and measuring risk

Investors require a return on the market value of their investment commensurate with the risk they cannot diversify away.

Consider two risks: the risk that a tornado destroys the manufacturing facilities of company A and the risk that a sudden and significant rise in the price of oil raises production costs throughout the economy. The first risk is *unsystematic, specific* and therefore *diversifiable*. A tornado might destroy a factory of company A but not one of company B. If, as an investor, we own equity in each company, we are partially protected against these firm-specific events, such as tornadoes, because they do not affect all companies. The second risk is *systematic, non-diversifiable* since the rise in oil prices will adversely affect all companies (with the exception of oil producers!). So we do not have a better protection against this risk if we hold equity in both companies A and B than if we just hold it in company A.

So we can diversify away unsystematic risk by investing in several different companies (empirical studies show that a portfolio made of

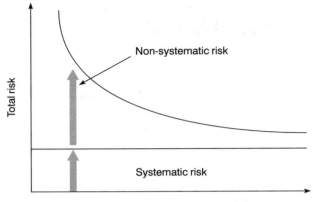

Figure 4.1   Thinking about risk

20 to 30 securities has very little unsystematic risk left) but we cannot
diversify away systematic risk because, by definition, it affects all
companies. This is shown in Figure 4.1.

In financial markets, investors are only rewarded for bearing
systematic risk because it is the only kind of risk that cannot be
diversified away. A method to measure systematic risk is to estimate
how much the returns of a company *covary* with the market returns.
The β coefficient measures systematic risk by estimating the covar-
iance of the firm returns with the market returns.[1]

A company whose returns exactly parallel the returns of the market
is exactly as risky as the market, it has a beta of one[2].

---

[1] Beta results from a regression of firm returns on markets returns. So the estimate of
β is equal to cov (firm return, market return) / variance (market return)

i.e. $\beta_i = \dfrac{\text{cov}(r_i,\ r_m)}{\text{var}(r_m)} = \dfrac{\sigma_{i,m}^2}{\sigma_m^2}$

which is equal to $\rho_{i,m}\ \dfrac{\sigma_i \sigma_m}{\sigma_m^2}$

where r_i = company i return,
        r_m = market return,
        $\sigma_{i,m}^2$ = covariance of firm returns with the market returns,
        σ_i = the standard deviation of the firm i returns,
        σ_m = the standard deviation of the market returns,
        $\rho_{i,m}$ = the correlation coefficient between the firm returns and the market
                 returns.

[2] Mathematically, if the returns of the firm and the returns of the market are the same,
then cov(r_i, r_m) = var (r_m)

so beta = $\dfrac{\text{var}(r_m)}{\text{var}(r_m)} = 1$

A company whose returns amplify the market's returns is riskier; it has a beta coefficient greater than one.

A company whose returns move less than the market's returns is less risky and has a beta smaller than one. Figure 4.2 summarizes these three cases and Tables 4.1, 4.2 and 4.3 provide some examples of beta coefficients computed for companies in the UK, France and Germany.

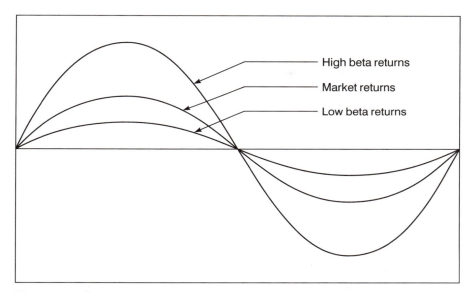

Figure 4.2 Summary of beta returns

Let us summarize the key points:

- Total risk = Unsystematic risk + Systematic risk
  (firm-specific risk)   (market risk or β risk)

- Examples of unsystematic risks are: death of the CEO, strike in the company, an R&D project fails, etc.
  Examples of systematic risks are: business cycles, inflation/recession, change in the tax system. . .

- What matters is not volatility *per se* (the standard deviation of stock returns) but correlation of firm returns with the market returns. β measures the risk left over once a portfolio is diversified.

- Investors are not compensated for risks they can eliminate themselves. The risk that they must be compensated for is systematic (β) risk.

Table 4.1   Beta coefficients for some UK companies

MCap rank, 31/12/98	Company	Beta	Source of beta
1	Glaxo Wellcome	0.88	DS (Datastream)
2	British Telecom	0.79	DS
3	BP Amoco	0.65	DS
4	Smithkline-Beecham	1.1	DS
5	Shell Transport & T	0.85	DS
6	Vodafone Group	1.19	DS
7	Zeneca	0.94	DS
8	Diageo	1.04	DS
9	Unilever (UK)	0.97	DS
10	Cable & Wireless	1.35	DS
11	BG	0.56	DS
12	General Electric	0.81	DS
13	Rentokil Initial	1.13	DS
14	Marks & Spencer	0.58	DS
15	Tesco	0.58	DS
16	Granada Group	1.14	DS
17	Boots	0.51	DS
18	Cadbury Schweppes	0.98	DS
19	Sainsbury (J)	0.19	DS
20	British Aerospace	1.22	DS
21	Reuters Group	1.16	DS
22	Kingfisher	0.59	DS
23	Orange	1.05	DS
24	British American Tobacco	0.69	DS
25	Cable & Wireless CC	0.79	Calculated
26	Railtrack Group	0.41	DS
27	British Sky Broadcasting	0.42	DS
28	BAA	0.97	DS
29	Rio Tinto	0.77	DS
30	Scottish Power	0.75	DS

Table 4.2 Beta coefficients for some French companies

MCap rank, 31/12/98	Company	Beta	Source of beta
1	France Telecom	1.500	DS
2	L'Oreal	1.229	DS
3	Vivendi (ex Generale des Eaux)	0.966	DS
4	Elf Aquitaine	0.654	DS
5	Suez Lyonnaise des Eaux	0.923	DS
6	Carrefour	0.762	DS
7	Total	0.508	DS
8	Alcatel Alsthom	1.438	DS
9	Pinault Printemps	1.108	DS
10	Danone	0.930	DS
11	Rhone Poulenc	1.140	DS
12	Sanofi	0.489	DS
13	LVMH	1.163	DS
14	Air Liquide	0.673	DS
15	Promodes	0.900	DS
16	Saint Gobain	1.069	DS
17	Stmicroelectronics	0.591	DS
18	Cap Gemini	0.770	DS
19	Renault	1.488	DS
20	Synthelabo	0.397	DS
21	Lafarge	0.985	DS
22	Schneider	1.448	DS
23	Canal +	0.425	DS
24	*Havas (acquired in May 1998)	0.891	DS
25	Accor	1.056	DS
26	Peugeot SA	1.091	DS
27	Casino Guipchn.	0.611	DS
28	Sodexho Alliance	0.272	DS
29	Thomson-CSF	1.094	DS
30	Valeo	1.168	DS

4.1.2 Applying CAPM to measure expected returns

CAPM specifies a simple linear relationship between risk and returns.[3]

$$E(R) = r_f + \beta(r_m - r_f)$$

where $E(R)$ is the expected return by investors, r_f is the risk-free rate of return, $\beta(r_m - r_f)$ is the risk premium demanded by investors and made of:

[3] It is not the purpose of this book to present in detail the CAPM and the assumptions on which this model relies. This can be found in any theoretical presentation of the Capital Asset Pricing Model.

- (r_m-r_f) the equity market risk premium, i.e. the returns expected on the market well-diversified portfolio, minus the risk-free rate of return. It represents the 'price of risk',
- β is the measure of the 'quantity of risk'.

At zero risk, investors can expect to earn the riskless rate of return r_f.

At higher levels of risk, investors expect in addition to the risk-free rate a risk premium, which depends upon the average risk premium

Table 4.3 Beta coefficients for some German companies

MCap rank, 31/12/98	Company	Beta	Source of beta
1	Deutsche Telekom	0.974	Calculated
2	SAP	1.014	DS
3	Mannesmann	1.263	DS
4	*Daimler-Benz	1.148	DS
5	Siemens	1.094	DS
6	RWE	0.847	DS
7	Bayer	1.059	DS
8	Veba	0.813	DS
9	Volkswagen	1.27	DS
10	Metro	0.445	Calculated
11	Hoechst	1.04	DS
12	BASF	1.043	DS
13	BMW	1.328	DS
14	Viag	0.681	DS
15	Henkel	1.112	DS
16	Schering	0.882	DS
17	Lufthansa	1.124	DS
18	Preussag	0.909	DS
19	Thyssen	0.981	DS
20	Beiersdorf	0.83	DS
21	Fresenius Medical Care	0.72	Calculated
22	Heidelberger Druckmaschine	0.698	Calculated
23	Linde	0.895	DS
24	Degussa	1.244	DS
25	GEHE	0.394	DS
26	Adidas Salomon AG	0.912	Calculated
27	Mobilcom	0.679	Calculated
28	Energie Baden Wuert.	0.168	DS
29	Lahmeyer AG	0.698	DS
30	Karstadt	0.577	DS

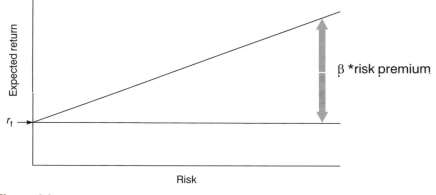

Figure 4.3

expected from the market multiplied by the amount of risk taken by the investors. Figure 4.3 shows a representation of the simple linear relationship between risk and return.

To estimate the components of CAPM, we need three pieces of information: r_f, β and (r_m-r_f):

- r_f: This is the yield on government bonds with maturities roughly equivalent to the cash flows being valued. So long-term rates will always be preferred to short-term rates on Treasury securities.
- β: To find β we can use linear regressions by regressing the excess returns on the stock $(r_{it}-r_{ft})$ on the market excess returns $(r_{mt}-r_{ft})$ when r_{it} represents the return on stock i at time t, r_{ft} the risk-free rate of return at time t and r_{mt} the return on the market at time t. Or better, let us not reinvent the wheel and let us use numerous sources of information providing these beta coefficients.[4]
- $(r_m - r_f)$: This equity market risk premium is estimated by using historical data. Unlike the risk-free rate, the risk premium is fairly stable over time. Table 4.4 shows the market risk premium for various European countries, with an average of about 6%. The level of the equity risk premium is the subject of much academic dispute and a growing concern among investment bankers, economic experts and financial journalists[5].

---

[4] These coefficients can be found, in the US, through Merryl Lynch Beta Box, Bloomberg, Value Line and many other sources. In Europe, Datastream, Barra International, Associes en Finance, . . . among others, are providing these beta coefficients.

[5] See 'Wall Street and the amazing vanishing risk premium', *Financial Times*, 22 April 1998; 'Risk premium paradox', *Financial Times*, 15 June 1998 and 'Calculated risks', *Financial Times* 3 May 1999.

Table 4.4 Cost of equity in Europe (%, as of close 04/02/99)

	IRR	10y bond yields	Risk premium	Adjusted volatility factor	Adjusted risk premium
Austria	10.3	3.9	6.4	1.35	8.6
Belgium	8.9	4.0	4.9	0.99	4.9
Denmark	8.9	4.2	4.7	1.04	4.9
Finland	9.7	4.0	5.7	1.00	5.7
France	9.1	3.9	5.2	1.00	5.2
Germany	9.0	3.8	5.3	0.97	5.1
Ireland	10.0	4.0	6.0	1.20	7.2
Italy	11.2	4.2	6.9	1.20	8.3
Netherlands	9.1	3.9	5.2	0.80	4.2
Norway	11.5	4.8	6.7	1.05	7.0
Portugal	10.8	4.3	6.5	1.20	7.8
Spain	9.2	4.0	5.2	1.07	5.6
Sweden	9.9	4.1	5.8	0.98	5.6
Switzerland	9.0	2.5	6.5	0.87	5.7
United Kingdom	10.5	4.2	6.2	0.72	4.5
Weighted average			5.8		5.3

Source: Credit Suisse First Boston (Europe) Limited (CSFB) estimates

4.2 Calculating the cost of capital

The cost of capital is derived from the basic linear relationship between risk and return that we have just reviewed. We can look at it in basically two ways depending upon which side of the balance sheet we are focusing.

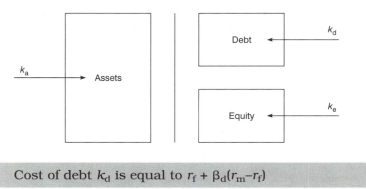

Cost of debt k_d is equal to $r_f + \beta_d(r_m - r_f)$

This is the expected rate of return required by investors holding the firm's debt.

> Cost of equity k_e is equal to $r_f + \beta_e(r_m - r_f)$

This is the expected rate of return by equity holders to compensate them for the opportunity cost of time and risk.

> Cost of assets k_a is equal to $r_f + \beta_a(r_m - r_f)$

This is the expected rate of return a company must generate to meet the return requirements of *all* providers of capital (debt capital and equity capital).

If we call D the market value of debt, E the market value of equity and V the total market value of the firm, we should obviously have the following relationship:

$$k_a = \frac{D}{V} k_d + \frac{E}{V} k_e \tag{1}$$

Given the fact that r_f and $(r_m - r_f)$ are the same for the three costs, we can easily derive the following formula

$$\beta_a = \frac{D}{V} \beta_d + \frac{E}{V} \beta_e \tag{2}$$

In other words, the asset β is a weighted average of the debt β and the equity β.

In practice, we tend to use the empirical fact that measured β_d's are quite small so that we assume that they are equal to zero, allowing equation (2) to be simplified to:

$$\beta_a = \frac{E}{V} \beta_e \tag{3}$$

The asset β (β_a) is sometimes referred to as the *unlevered beta* and shown as β_u in some calculations. The equity β (β_e) is, in the same way, referred to as the *levered beta* and shown as β_L. Therefore, unlevering an equity beta (or a levered beta) to get an asset beta (or an

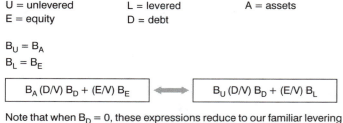

U = unlevered   L = levered   A = assets
E = equity   D = debt

$B_U = B_A$
$B_L = B_E$

$$\boxed{B_A \, (D/V) \, B_D + (E/V) \, B_E} \longleftrightarrow \boxed{B_U \, (D/V) \, B_D + (E/V) \, B_L}$$

Note that when $B_D = 0$, these expressions reduce to our familiar levering and unlevering formulas:

$B_A = (E/V) \, B_E \longleftrightarrow B_U = (E/V) \, B_L$

$K_U = R_F + B_U \, (R_M - R_F) \longleftrightarrow K_A = R_F + B_A \, (R_M - R_F)$

$$\boxed{K_U = D/V \, K_D + E/V \, K_E, \text{ which is similar to WACC, without tax shield}}$$

Figure 4.4   Terminology and mathematical relations

unlevered beta) requires the ratio between the equity value and the value of the firm measured in market value terms.[6]

When a company has no debt, i.e. is unlevered, its asset beta is obviously equal to its equity beta. All this terminology and mathematical relations are summarized in Figure 4.4.

Let us illustrate these various relations by a simple example. Company X has the following balance sheet (in millions €) in market values.

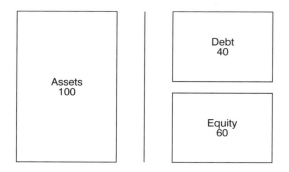

Assets
100

Debt
40

Equity
60

R_f is equal to 5% and the equity market premium is assumed to be 6%. Company X has an equity β of 1.3 and borrows money at r_f (which means that the debt is riskless and βd = 0).

---

[6] Often, capital structure will be provided to you on a book value basis. Typically, in most cases, we assume that the book value of debt is equal to its market value but that is not plausible for equity. The market value of equity may be calculated as PER (price earnings ratio) × net profit.

The cost of equity k_e is equal to: $5\% + 1.3(6\%) = 12.8\%$

The 'blended' cost of capital[7]

$$\frac{D}{V} k_d + \frac{E}{V} k_e$$

is therefore equal to

$$40\% \times 5\% + 60\% \times 12.8\% = \mathbf{9.68\%}$$

By unlevering the equity β, using equation (3), we can find the asset β

$$\beta_a = \frac{E}{V} \beta_e \Rightarrow \beta_a = 60\% \times 1.3 = 0.78$$

The cost of assets k_a is equal to

$$k_a = r_f + \beta_a (r_m - r_f)$$
$$= 5\% + 0.78(6\%) = \mathbf{9.68\%}$$

4.2.1 The weighted average cost of capital (WACC) approach: looking at the right-hand side of the balance sheet

WACC is directly derived from the blended requirements of both lenders and shareholders of equation (1), taking into account the tax deductibility of interests. If the company is profitable and the tax rate in decimals is t, the after-tax cost of debt k_d^{AT} will be equal to k_d (the cost of debt before tax shields provided by interest) multiplied by $(1 - t)$. Therefore WACC is given by the following formula:

$$\mathrm{WACC} = \frac{D}{V} k_d(1 - t) + \frac{E}{V} k_e \qquad (4)$$

[7] We use this expression 'blended' cost of capital to distinguish it from the weighted average cost of capital which, as shown in the next section, takes taxes into consideration.

One important thing to keep in mind is that k_d and k_e are numbers associated with a specific capital structure. This simply means that k_d and k_e are functions of the proportion of debt and equity. So, whatever capital structure one uses, one needs to be consistent and to use the k_d and k_e corresponding to that same capital structure. When calculating a company WACC, we will use the firm's *target* capital structure, that is the capital structure the company is aiming at or committed to maintain over time, measured in market values. Therefore, in equation (4)

$\dfrac{D}{V}$ is the percentage of debt in the firm's target capital structure, calculated with market values

$\dfrac{E}{V}$ is the percentage of equity in the firm's target capital structure, calculated with market values

k_d is the expected rate of return required by investors holding the firm's debt (lenders, bondholders . . .)

k_e is the expected rate of return required by equity investors

t is the corporate tax rate[8]

The WACC is calculated for the example in the previous section, assuming a 40% marginal tax rate

$$\text{WACC} = 40\% \times 5\%[0.6] + 60\% \times 12.8\% = 8.88\%$$

The difference between 8.88% and the 9.68% we found for k_a earlier measures the impact of tax shields provided by the interest payments on debt.

Estimating k_d is usually not a problem. It is an explicit cost, a contractual commitment and it is rather straightforward to assess the rate the firm will pay on future debt issues.

We should note that this rate is what the company *promises* to pay in its debt, which is not exactly the same as the rate debt holders *expect*. By using this promised return as a proxy for expected returns, we are implicitly assuming that the probability of the company defaulting on its debt is quite low (which is a reasonable assumption when debt is investment-grade).

---

[8] By taking on additional debt, a corporation is shielding income from taxes. Without that debt, it would pay tax at the *marginal tax rate* on that income. t should therefore be the marginal tax rate, i.e. the amount of tax a company pays on the last euro of income it earned. The *average tax rate* is the amount of tax a corporation paid on average across all euros it earned.

To measure the equity holders' expected return, we use the Capital Asset Pricing Model:

$$k_e = r_f + \beta_e (r_m - r_f)$$

which is easy as long as the company's equity is traded on the stock market and we can calculate or get a value for β_e. If we are considering a privately held company, a business unit, or part of a holding company, we have to rely on comparable 'pure play' firms for which we can get measures of beta coefficients. These coefficients reflect the basic business risk and the financial risk. If we have selected our 'pure play' firms in the same industries and businesses that the company or the business unit we are trying to value, the basic business risk can be assumed to be similar. But what if the financial risk, i.e. the debt structure, is different. Then we need first to unlever the β of our 'pure play' firms to get an unlevered β or an asset β and relever it using the target financial structure of our company.

Let us illustrate this methodology with a simple example.

You are thinking of buying a privately held company that has a ratio of debt to total capital of 20%. There is a similar company, with the same type of business and therefore the same basic business risk, with a beta of 1.8 and a debt ratio of 50%.[9] The risk free rate is 5% and the equity-market risk premium is 6% and you are wondering which cost of equity you should use when evaluating the WACC relevant for the valuation of the privately held company.

The *first step* is to unlever the comparable beta using equation (3)

$$\beta_a = \frac{E}{V} \beta_e$$

If $\dfrac{D}{V}$ is 0.5 (50%), $\dfrac{E}{V}$ is equal to 0.5 too.

$$\Rightarrow \beta_a = 1.8 \times 0.5 = 0.9$$

This means that unlevered companies in this type of business have a β of 0.9.

---

[9] We assume that the debt ratios are given in *market* values.

The *second step* is to relever this unlevered β using the capital structure of our target company. Equation (3) can be written as

$$\beta_e = \beta_a \frac{V}{E} \qquad\qquad (4)$$

Using equation (4), we derive the equity β of the privately-held company, with

$$\frac{V}{E} = 1.25 \left(\text{if } \frac{D}{V} = 0.2 \Rightarrow \frac{E}{V} = 0.8 \Rightarrow \frac{V}{E} = \frac{1}{0.8} = 1.25 \right)$$

$$\beta_e = 0.9 \times 1.25 = 1.13$$

The third step, using the equity beta of 1.13, is to calculate the cost of equity (k_e) relevant to the privately-held company

$$k_e = 5\% + 1.13\,(6\%) = 11.78\%$$

If, as an investor, we are investing equity capital in this privately held company, we should expect a return on our investment close to 11.8%.

We have used, as we do in practice, the simplified formula for unlevering and relevering (equations (3) and (4)) which assume that the debt is riskless ($\beta_d = 0$), and that the value of debt is proportional to the total value of the firm, which means that the firm varies the amount of debt outstanding in each period following the change in its total value.[10]

---

[10] Richard S. Ruback has shown in various papers, in particular 'Capital cash flows: a simple approach to valuing risky cash flows,' Harvard Business School, Working Paper April 1998, that the standard unlevering and levering formula should include tax effects when debt is assumed to be fixed (i.e. a fixed Euro amount). In that case, and still assuming that the debt is riskless ($\beta_d = 0$), the unlevering equation (3) becomes

$$\beta_e = \frac{E + D(1-t)}{E}\,\beta_a, \quad \text{where } t \text{ is the tax rate.}$$

If the debt is not riskless ($\beta_d > 0$), the formula becomes more complicated.

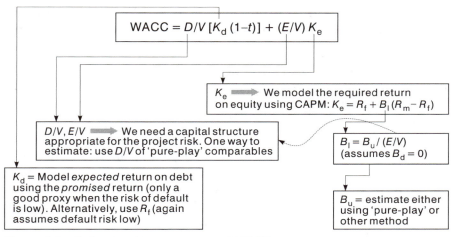

Figure 4.5 Estimating the components of WACC

Figure 4.5 summarizes the various components of WACC. To use WACC, remember the following hints:

- Assume *stable capital structure* with the firm following a proportional capital structure, i.e. D/V remains constant (if the firm market value increases by 50%, the amount of debt will increase by 50%).
- Cost of debt (k_d) and cost of equity (k_e) are *constant* and remain *unchanged* as long as D/V stays the same.
- When measuring D/V and E/V, use *market* weights.
- The firm is actually at its target capital structure[11] and is able to pay the promised interest (if a firm is levered to the extent that the debt has substantial default risk, then the promised k_d will substantially overstate the expected k_d).
- The tax rate is constant and the firm can use its interest tax shield in the year it occurs.
- The rate the firm pays on its debt represents a market rate (as opposed to a subsidized rate which is sometimes current practice in some industries and in some countries).

We should not forget that, as we move away from these assumptions, WACC becomes very risky to use and the modifications to make it work properly are likely to be complicated.

---

[11] There are clearly categories of firms for which this is not the case. For example, firms undergoing leverage buyouts (LBOs) have levered themselves to the top and then pay down the debt over several years, before reaching a stable capital structure.

4.2.2 The asset cost of capital, or the unlevered cost of capital: looking at the left-hand side of the balance sheet

Since we are evaluating assets, why don't we discount the cash flows expected from the assets at an unlevered cost of capital and calculate the tax shield from interests as a separate component? This is the basis for the APV (adjusted present value) method described in the next chapter.

If asset betas were given to us, this method would be a major improvement since we would not have to worry about the financial structure of the firm and we would only concentrate on the left-hand side of the balance sheet, i.e. the asset side. Unfortunately, we seldom observe asset betas as the assets and their cash flows don't trade in markets in any observable way. Equities trade as securities on financial markets and therefore we observe equity betas. Unlevering equity betas using equation (3) allows us to get asset betas (or, as we call them sometimes, unlevered betas).

Table 4.5 demonstrates the relationship between WACC and k_a (the unlevered or the asset cost of capital) which provides a simplifying way to calculate WACC and therefore a useful method to approximate it.

4.3 Single versus multiple cost of capital

Whether we are using WACC or k_a, the key question is: should we have a single company-wide cost of capital or individual costs of capital for each line of business?

From an outsider point of view, the investors, there should be one single cost of capital reflecting the required rate of return for the capital suppliers (debtholders and stockholders for WACC, stockholders for k_a) commensurate with the risk that they are taking when investing their funds in the company as a whole and ensuring that the various investments will achieve the goal of value maximization.

From an internal point of view, the resource allocation process between various parts of the company, the rationale is different. 'The major consequence of using a single cut-off criterion for all projects is an intra-firm misallocation of capital, since the acceptance rule is biased in favour of the acceptance of high-risk projects. Thus, low-risk divisions may be starved for capital in spite of their ability to generate proposals offering returns in excess of those required for the systematic risk involved. The ultimate consequence of such misallocation of capital is a reduction of shareholder wealth.'[12] This can be shown by the graph on Figure 4.6.

---

[12] 'Divisional cost of equity capital', James DeBono, *Management Accounting*, November 1997 p. 40.

Table 4.5 Relationship between WACC and k_a

From CAPM $\quad k_e = r_f + \beta_e (r_m - r_f)$

$\Rightarrow k_e - r_f = \beta_e (r_m - r_f)$ (1')

and $\quad\quad\quad k_a = r_f + \beta_a (r_m - r_f)$

$\Rightarrow k_a - r_f = \beta_a (r_m - r_f)$ (2')

Dividing (1') by (2')

$$\frac{k_e - r_f}{k_a - r_f} = \frac{\beta_e (r_m - r_f)}{\beta_a (r_m - r_f)}$$

$\Rightarrow k_e - r_f = \beta_e/\beta_a (k_a - r_f)$ (3')

From equation (3)

$$\beta_a = \frac{E}{V} \beta_e \Rightarrow \frac{\beta_a}{\beta_e} = \frac{E}{V}$$

$$\Rightarrow \frac{\beta_e}{\beta_a} = \frac{V}{E}$$

$$\Rightarrow k_e - r_f = \frac{V}{E} (k_a - r_f) \quad \text{or} \quad \frac{E}{V} (k_e - r_f) = (k_a - r_f)$$

$$\Rightarrow \frac{E}{V} k_e = \frac{E}{V} r_f + (k_a - r_f)$$ (4')

$$\frac{E}{V} k_e = k_a - r_f \left(1 - \frac{E}{V}\right)$$ (5')

since by definition $\left(1 - \dfrac{E}{V}\right) = \dfrac{D}{V}$

(5') may be re-written as:

$$\frac{E}{V} k_e = k_a - \frac{D}{V} r_f$$ (6')

the formula for WACC given by (4)

$$\text{WACC} = \frac{D}{V} k_d (1 - t) + \frac{E}{V} k_e$$

Substituting (6') into (4) leads to

$$\text{WACC} = \frac{D}{V} k_d (1 - t) + k_a - \frac{D}{V} r_f$$ (7')

Table 4.5   (*Continued*)

Collecting terms in $\dfrac{D}{V}$

$$\text{WACC} = k_a + \underbrace{\frac{D}{V}[k_d(1-t) - r_f]}$$ (8')

           This term, particularly for low debt ratios,
           is very small and can be neglected

Therefore

$$\text{WACC} = k_a$$

If r_f is 5%,

and a company with a $\dfrac{D}{V}$ of 20% borrows at 7% and has a marginal tax rate of 40%,

$\dfrac{D}{V}[k_d(1-t) - r_f]$ would be equal to: $0.20[0.07(0.6) - 0.05] = 0.0016$
                                            that is 0.16%

If we assume, as earlier, that the debt is riskless, i.e. that $\beta_d = 0$ and therefore $k_d = r_f$ then (8') would become

$$\text{WACC} = k_a + \frac{D}{V}[r_f(1-t) - r_f]$$

$$\Rightarrow \text{WACC} = k_a - tr_f\frac{D}{V}$$ (9')

with $r_f = 5\%$, $t = 40\%$,   and $\dfrac{D}{V} = 20\%$

$tr_f\dfrac{D}{V}$ would be $0.4 \times 0.05 \times 0.2 = 0.004$
                                 that is 0.4%

still a good approximation of WACC by k_a.

Despite a return higher than the company-wide cost of capital, Project B does not look to generate a profitability commensurate to the risk it is adding to the overall risk of the firm. Conversely, Project A which is not returning the average company cost of capital has a very low risk and a potentially attractive risk-return profile. In fact, following our previous discussion of the risk-return relationship, the graph should be as shown in Figure 4.7.

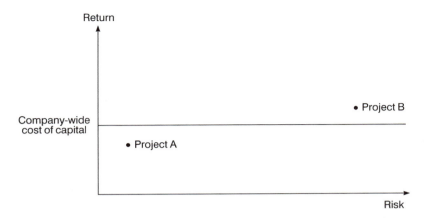

Figure 4.6

This graph illustrates the fact that Project A is financially attractive since its return is above the discount rate reflecting its risk character-istics, while Project B has a return far below what investors should expect from it given its riskiness. So, we should calculate a cost of capital (whether WACC or k_a) on a project basis. In practice this is an

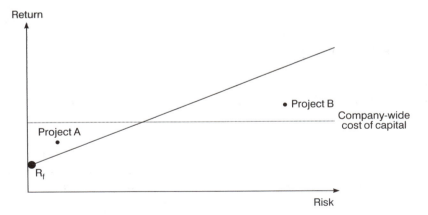

Figure 4.7

impossible task and we are going to approximate the risk-return line by a step function by classifying projects in different risk-classes, usually strategic business units, or divisions, or any other kind of sub-units. The graph thus becomes as shown in Figure 4.8 if we assume, for example, three risk levels.

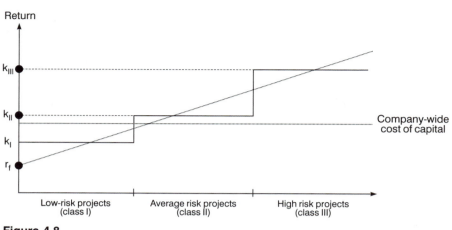

Figure 4.8

'The main problem with the calculation of divisional discount rates is the availability of information . . . The market data required does not exist for a non-traded firm or for a division of a publicly traded firm.'[13] One possible approach to deal with this difficulty is to use comparable 'pure-play' firms, with publicly traded securities, which are engaged solely in the same line of business as the division. According to different surveys, it seems that the use of risk-adjusted discount rates in the USA is gradually catching on, progressively reducing the gap between theory and practice, while in Europe it remains a completely new area.[14]

4.4 The cost of capital in an international framework

Globalization is reducing the cost of capital, the general argument being that, when barriers to international investment segment a domestic capital market from global capital markets, local investors bear all the risk of the economic activities in their economy. 'Such investors require a higher risk premium that effectively reduces the value that local investors are willing to place on the stock relative to

---

[13] Ibid.

[14] See in particular the survey conducted in 1996 by R.W. Mills, J.D. DeBono, U.D. DeBono, C. Print and D. Parker on the top 250 UK companies, reporting that 71% of responding firms utilized a company-wide discount rate and only the remaining 29% used divisional discount rates. 'The use of shareholder value analysis in acquisition and divestment decisions by large UK companies', Research Report for the Chartered Institute of Management Accountants, 1996.

what a globally diversified investor would pay if given the chance.'[15] Besides reducing market risk premiums, gaining access to global markets also reduces the Betas of most companies, particularly companies whose activity is more strongly correlated with their local economies than with the global economy. Empirical evidence is generally consistent with what the theory describes. Using monthly data for the period 1975–1997, Ronald M. Schramm and Henry N. Wong found that the estimated betas and costs of capital are significantly lower, on average, in integrated markets than in segmented markets. 'The average difference is 0.104 for beta and 31 basis points for the cost of capital.'[16]

Despite these findings (and many others in the financial literature), 'the financial management practices of many multinational corporations are decidedly at odds with both financial theory and the strategic case for globalism . . . many financial executives tend to require large premiums for making foreign investments, while ignoring the diversification benefits of such investments for their shareholders.'[17]

4.5 The use of cost of capital in measuring value creation: the concept of economic value added (EVA)

Economic Value Added (EVA) is becoming a more and more common tool for European executives to align corporate objectives and decision-making with shareholders' interests. EVA[18] measures the spread between return on capital employed and cost of capital. Economists will recognize this 'new' approach as nothing more than the economic profit described more than a century ago by Alfred Marshall. 'The value of economic profit is to remind managers that they have not really made a profit until they have earned an economic return on the capital they use.'[19] In other words, ROCE has to be higher than cost of capital.

[15] Stulz, Rene M. 'Globalization, corporate finance, and the cost of capital', *Journal of Applied Corporate Finance*, Volume 12, Number 3, Fall 1999, p. 10.
[16] Schramm, Ronald M. and Henry N. Wong, 'Measuring the cost of capital in an international CAPM framework', *Journal of Applied Corporate Finance*, Volume 12, Number 3, Fall 1999, p. 68.
[17] Pettit, Justin, Mack, Ferguson and Robert Gluck 'A method for estimating global corporate capital costs: the case of Bestfoods,' *Journal of Applied Corporate Finance*, Volume 12, Number 3, Fall 1999, p. 90.
[18] EVA is actually Stern Stewart & Co's trade name for a specific method of calculating economic profit, which includes capital charges and a long list of accounting adjustments.
[19] De-jargoning EVA, by John Rutledge, Forbes, Oct. 25, 1993 p. 148.

4.5.1 *Definitions*

ROCE is defined as earnings before interests and after taxes (EBIAT)[20] divided by capital employed which is defined either as net fixed assets + net operating working capital or net financial debt + book value of equity. Figure 4.9 and 4.10 summarize the definitions of EBIAT and capital employed.

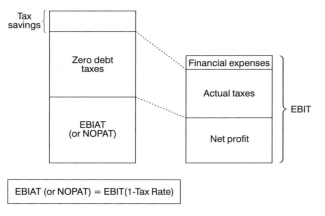

EBIAT (or NOPAT) = EBIT(1-Tax Rate)

= EBIT - Zero debt taxes (i.e. taxes as if the firm has no debt)

In fact Actual taxes = Zero debt taxes – Tax savings

Savings in taxes due to tax deductibility of interests

Figure 4.9   Net profit, EBIT and EBIAT (or NOPAT)

In order for a company, or any business unit, to create value, the return on capital employed has to be greater than (or at least equal to) the cost of the capital supplied by the various capital providers.

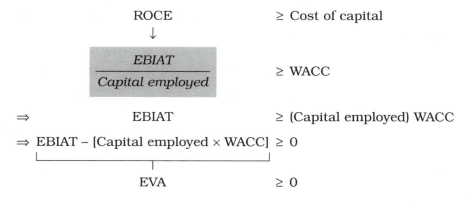

[20] This EBIAT is sometimes referred to as NOPAT (net operating profit after taxes)

Traditional B/S

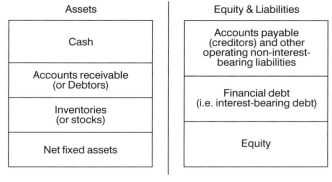

Assets = Equity + Liabilities

Cash + A/R + Inventories + NFA = A/P and other accruals + Financial debt + Equity

A/R + Inventories – A/P & other accruals + NFA = Financial debt – Cash + Equity

Net operating working capital   Net financial debt

Net operating working capital + NFA = Net financial debt + Equity

Capital employed   Capital employed

Revised B/S

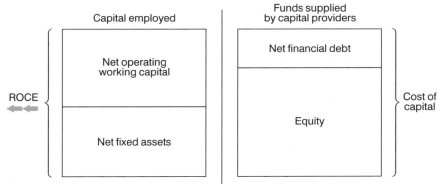

Figure 4.10 From total assets to capital employed

If EVA is bigger than zero, the firm, or the business unit, is earning more than its weighted average cost of capital, and therefore is unique in the sense that the capital providers could not have got that performance elsewhere. There is value creation.

If EVA is equal to zero, the firm, or the business unit, is just earning its cost of capital, which means that it is just 'doing its job', the capital providers could have got exactly the same result elsewhere, for the same level of risk.

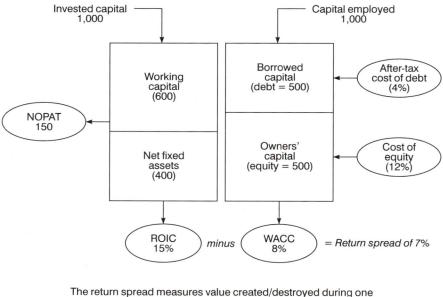

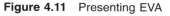

The return spread measures value created/destroyed during one
year for the use of *one* euro of capital

EVA measures the same for *total* capital employed capital:

EVA = (ROIC – WACC) × invested capital

EVA = (15% – 8%) × 1,000 = 70

which can also be written as:

EVA = NOPAT – WACC × invested capital

EVA = €150 – 8% × 1,000 = €150 – €80 = 70

Figure 4.11   Presenting EVA

If EVA is less than zero, the firm, or the business unit, is not earning
its cost of capital. Capital providers would have been able to get a
better return elsewhere, for the given level of risk. There is value
destruction.

Figure 4.11 summarizes the two ways of presenting EVA, together
with a simple example.

4.6 The use of cost of capital and EVA in understanding financial policies: the example of share repurchases

'The only sensible strategy for businesses that generate a lot of cash
and find themselves sitting on a mountain of excess capital is to

return the money to shareholders, who are not employing and paying talented managers to invest surplus of cash in short term securities. Buying back its shares appears as one of the most effective methods of using excess financial capacity to drive shareholder value.'[21] A simple example will illustrate this fact. Let us assume a company with the following balance sheet:

Assets		*Equity and liabilities*	
Cash	€100$_m$		
A/R	€200$_m$	A/P	€100$_m$
Investors	€150$_m$	Financial debt	€200$_m$
NFA	€250$_m$	Equity	€400$_m$
	700$_m$		700$_m$

This balance sheet can be restated in the following way.

Cash	100$_m$	Financial debt	200$_m$
Capital employed	500$_m$	Equity	400$_m$

Capital employed = NFA + Net operating working capital

$$= 250_m + [200_m + 150_m - 100_m] = 500_m$$

The ROCE is assumed to be 12%, Cost of equity 10% and After tax cost of debt 4%.

WACC is therefore equal to $\left[\left(\dfrac{2}{3} \times 10\%\right) + \left(\dfrac{1}{3} \times 4\%\right)\right] = 8\%$

ROCE − WACC = 12% − 8% = 4%

$\Rightarrow$ EVA = 500$_m$ × 0.04 = 20$_m$ [22]

We assume, as shown previously, that

Market value of equity = equity + Present value of EVA

Firm value = Market value of debt + Market value of equity

Shareholder value = Market value of equity + Cash paid to shareholders

[21] Bertoneche, M. 'Share buy backs: the European and Japanese experience', Harvard Business School, note 9.298.134 p. 2.
[22] Or, alternatively, EBIAT is 12% of capital employed of 500$_m$

i.e.: 60$_m$.

$\Rightarrow$ EVA = 60$_m$ − [500$_m$ × 0.08] = 20$_m$ €.

Case 1   Cash is kept in the balance sheet and invested on the money market at an after-tax rate of 2%

$$\text{EVA of Cash} = 100_m^- \ [0.02 - 0.08] = -6_m^- €$$

The return on cash is value destructive

$$\text{Total EVA} = €20_m^- - €6_m^- = €14_m^-$$

Present value of EVA, assuming a constant perpetuity,[23] is $14_m^-/0.08$ $= 175_m^- €$.

Therefore Market value of equity $= 400_m^- + 175_m^- = 575_m^-$

$\Rightarrow$ Value of the firm $= 575_m^- + 200_m^- = 775_m^-$

and Shareholder value $= 575 + 0 = \underline{575_m^- €}$

Case 2   Cash is used to pay down debt, since there are no profitable opportunities to invest cash

After 100_m^- of debt repayment, the balance sheet becomes:

			Net financial debt	100_m^-
Capital employed	$\dfrac{500_m^-}{500_m^-}$		Equity	$\dfrac{400_m^-}{500_m^-}$

WACC becomes in that case, assuming for simplicity no changes in cost of equity and cost of debt:

$$\left(\frac{4}{5} \times 10\%\right) + \left(\frac{1}{5} \times 4\%\right) = 8.8\%$$

$$\text{ROCE} - \text{WACC} = 12\% - 8.8\% = 3.2\%$$

EVA on total capital employed $= 500_m^- \times 3.2\% = \boldsymbol{16_m^-}$

---

[23] Recall that a constant flow X forever (i.e. a constant perpetuity), when the cost of capital is k, is worth X/k. A review of the perpetuity formulae is done in the next chapter.

Present value of EVA, assuming a constant perpetuity,

$$\frac{16\overline{}_m}{0.088} = 181.8\overline{}_m$$

Market value of equity $= 400\overline{}_m + 181.8\overline{}_m = 581.8\overline{}_m$

$\Rightarrow$ Value of the firm $= 581.8\overline{}_m + 100\overline{}_m = 681.8\overline{}_m$

Shareholder value $= 581.8\overline{}_m + 0 = 581.8\overline{}_m$

Case 3   Excess cash can be invested at a return higher than WACC, for example at 10%, but below existing return on capital employed (12%)

EVA of Invested Cash $= 100\overline{}_m [0.10{-}0.08] = 2\overline{}_m€$

The return on invested cash is creating value since it is above WACC
   Total EVA for the firm is therefore in that case

$€20\overline{}_m + 2\overline{}_m = €22\overline{}_m$

Present value of EVA, still assuming a constant perpetuity,

$$\frac{€22\overline{}_m}{0.08} = 275\overline{}_m€$$

Market value of equity $= 400\overline{}_m + 275\overline{}_m = 675\overline{}_m$

Value of the firm $= 100\overline{}_m + 675\overline{}_m = 775\overline{}_m$

Shareholder value $= 675\overline{}_m + 0 = \mathbf{675\overline{}_m€}$

Case 4   Cash is returned to shareholders through share buy-backs (or special dividends) because no profitable investment opportunities can be found

Equity is reduced to 400 m – 100 m = 300 m and the balance sheet has now the following mix:

		Financial debt	200_m
Capital employed	$\dfrac{500_\text{m}}{500_\text{m}}$	Equity	$\dfrac{300_\text{m}}{500_\text{m}}$

WACC becomes, assuming again for simplicity no changes in the cost of equity and the cost of debt

$$[\tfrac{3}{5} \times 10\%] + [\tfrac{2}{5} \times 4\%] = 7.6\%$$

$$\text{ROCE} - \text{WACC} = 12\% - 7.6\% = 4.4\%$$

EVA of total capital employed $= 500_\text{m} \times 0.044 = 22_\text{m}$

$$\text{Present value of EVA} = \frac{22_\text{m}}{0.076} = 289.5_\text{m}€$$

Market value of Equity 300_m $+ 289.5_\text{m} = 589.5_\text{m}$

Firm value: 200_m $+ 589.5_\text{m} = 789.5_\text{m}$

Shareholder value: $589.5_\text{m} + 100_\text{m}$ $= 689.5_\text{m}$

The share buy-back (or distribution of a special dividend) is creating value and shows the highest record for shareholder value. As long as excess cash cannot be invested at a return higher that the WACC, this policy leads to the best result.[24]

So, cost of capital is an essential concept in management. Whatever function we are in, we have to understand it and know it. From the company perspective, it is a resource cost, WACC being to capital what wages are to labour. From the investor perspective, it compensates them for the opportunity cost of time and risk what they could get elsewhere from comparable investments in the same class of risk.

---

[24] The increased financial leverage has the positive consequence of reducing the weighted average cost of capital. We have assumed, for simplicity, that the cost of equity is not affected by the operation and remains unchanged.

5

Valuation: principles and methods

The value of any asset, tangible or intangible, commercial, industrial or financial, is the present value of the expected stream of cash flows from this asset at the cost of capital.

The formula is therefore:

$$V = \frac{CF_1}{(1 + k)} + \frac{CF_2}{(1 + k)^2} + \ldots + \frac{CF_n}{(1+k)^n} \tag{1}$$

in which

- CF are the cash flows available to the investors (shareholders and lenders) who financed the asset;
- k is the opportunity cost of capital. This is the return that investors can get from alternative investments in the same risk class as the asset (see Chapter 4);
- n is the expected economic life of the asset.

5.1 The basic discounted cash flow (DCF) approach: a simple example

This basic and fundamental principle can be illustrated by a very simple example.

Let us assume that you have decided to buy an apartment not to live in it but to rent it, as an investment. You have prepared forecasts, in Euros, of the annual rent expected from this apartment in the next three years, the period over which you intend to keep the flat, and the resale value at the end of year 3.

	Year 1	*Year 2*	*Year 3*
Rent	10,000	10,500	11,000
Resale value			180,000

Based on the fact that you require a minimum return of 8%, reflecting the rate you can expect to earn by investing in alternative, identically risky assets, how much should you pay for your apartment today?

The answer to this very simple problem is straightforward:

10,000 Euros expected one year from now are worth for you $\dfrac{10,000}{(1+0.08)}$

i.e. €9259[1] today since investing €9259 at your opportunity cost of money (8%) for one year would provide you with exactly €10,000 one year from now.

By the same token, €10,500 expected at the end of the year (we assume that your tenant will pay you at the end of each year) is worth today:

$\dfrac{10,500}{(1+0.08)^2}$ i.e. €9002

If today you have €9002 and are able to invest this amount at 8% for two years, you know you would get €10,500 at the end of year 2.

'A bird in the hand is worth two in the bush' says the popular motto. Financially, a Euro in the bank is worth more than a Euro which you will receive in a year's time, simply because if you had it today you could use it to make more money in a year's time.

Discounting, as we call it, is a method for translating future values into present values in order to enable apples-to-apples comparisons.

Finally €11,000 due in three years is worth today

$\dfrac{11,000}{(1 + 0.08)^3}$ i.e. €8732

If we assume that you would be selling your apartment at the end of year 3, just after your three-year contract with your tenant had expired, the expected €180,000 resale price would be equal to €142,890 in today's money.

At that stage, you have the answer to your basic question: the value of this apartment for you, given your assumptions, is : €9259 + €9002 +

[1] This is a rounded figure.

€8732 + €142,890 i.e. €169,883. This simply means that if you pay €169,883 for your flat and if your forecasts happen to be exactly right, your investment will provide you with a return just equal to 8%, meeting your initial requirement. If you are lucky enough and can pay less than €169,883 for this apartment, you would generate for yourself a return higher than the required 8%.

If, on the contrary, you have to pay more than €169,883 to acquire the apartment, your rate of return will be lower than 8%. This seems quite obvious, but this is the basis for understanding valuation of assets. If, now, you have to evaluate a brand, or a business unit, or a full company, you will use the same methodology, even if the various parameters (cash flows, resale value, cost of capital, etc.) might be more difficult to predict.

Statistics and empirical studies suggest high failure rates of mergers and acquisitions all over the world. There are numerous reasons but the most likely is that acquirers pay too much. First, acquirers often are overoptimistic in their assumptions and estimations of the potential synergies (the managerial word for dreams!) If you start to be completely unrealistic about the rent you can expect from your apartment, no doubt that you will be willing to pay more. The second reason for overpaying is simply the fact that many companies, especially in Europe, have underestimated their cost of capital, by systematically underevaluating the cost of equity capital. Being too optimistic at the numerator level of the DCF formula and minimizing the discount rate at the denominator level is the best recipe to overvalue any asset.

5.2 Investment decision techniques

Coming back to your real estate investment, let us assume that you know the price of the apartment, which is €150,000, and there is no way you can negotiate it. If you keep the same assumptions for rents and terminal value over the next three years, we have calculated that this apartment is worth for you, today, €169,883. By paying €150,000, you would generate a surplus of €19,883 in today's money, which we call the net present value (NPV) of the investment project. Therefore NPV is the difference between present value of expected cash flows and present value of initial investment:

$$NPV = \frac{CF_1}{1 + k} + \frac{CF_2}{(1 + k)^2} + \ldots + \frac{CF_n}{(1 + k)^n} - I_0 \qquad (2)$$

The rule is simple:

- If a project has a positive NPV, it creates value and should be accepted.
- If it has a negative NPV, it destroys value and should be rejected.

NPV incorporates the magnitude, the timing and the risk of expected future cash flows. It is the most accurate investment decision criterion. Very often in practice, people tend to prefer internal rate of return (IRR) which apparently is more meaningful and appealing.

If you have a hard time understanding that by paying €150,000 for your apartment and assuming that all your forecasts are right, you would generate the minimum required rate of return of 8% plus a surplus spread over the life of your investment which today is worth €19,883, you might prefer to know what the rate of return is on your investment. You would do that by asking yourself which rate you should put in the DCF formula so that you find exactly €150,000. In other words, IRR is the rate which makes the present value of expected cash flows equal to the present value of initial investment (or to say it another way the rate at which NPV is equal to 0)

$$I_0 = \frac{CF_1}{(1 + IRR)} + \frac{CF_2}{(1 + IRR)^2} + \ldots + \frac{CF_n}{(1 + IRR)^n}$$

or

$$\frac{CF_1}{(1 + IRR)} + \frac{CF^2}{(1 + IRR)^2} + \ldots + \frac{CF_n}{(1 + IRR)^n} - I_0 = 0$$

Applying the formula to calculate the IRR of your real estate investment, you would find 12.85%, which is significantly higher than your minimum required rate of 8% and therefore confirms that your investment, given your assumptions, is financially attractive.

The rule, again, is simple:

- If an investment project has an IRR higher than the minimum required rate, the investment should be accepted.
- If, on the contrary, the IRR is less than the minimum required rate, the investment should be rejected.

IRR, generally, gives the correct accept–reject decision if used carefully but it often gives incorrect rankings for mutually exclusive projects, particularly if they differ in scale (amount of initial investment) or economic life and it suffers from various pitfalls (multiple IRR in some cases, when, for example, cash flows change signs, reinvestment assumption for cash flows at an IRR which might in many instances be very unrealistic, etc.)[2].

The lesson is straightforward: do not use IRR, use NPV instead. After all, we are not in business to maximize rate of return but to maximize value creation and what counts is the impact of a project on the wealth of shareholders, which is what NPV is measuring.

5.3 The parameters for valuation in the DCF approach

When you were wondering how much you should pay for your apartment, you needed four pieces of information: the expected cash flows, the time frame, the resale value (or terminal value) and the minimum required rate. We have, in the previous chapter, covered the cost of capital which, we have shown, is the minimum rate required for a given project. As far as the time horizon is concerned, it really depends upon the type of assets we are valuing, our ability to forecast and the available information. Table 5.1 summarizes some important facts to consider in choosing the length of the time horizon. We are going to concentrate, in this section, on the two remaining crucial parameters: the expected cash flows and the terminal value.

Table 5.1   Important facts to consider in choosing the length of the forecast period

---

The forecast period should be equal to the length of time management expects new investment rates of return to exceed the cost of capital

Management's expected value-creation period may differ from:

- the stock market's expected value-creation period
- management's normal planning period

Management should consider the following factors when estimating the value-creation period:

- Proprietary technologies
- Patented products
- Product life cycles
- Established brands
- Distribution channels

---

[2] It is not the purpose of this book to describe in details the various pitfalls of IRR. This can be found in any book on capital budgeting.

5.3.1 The appropriate expected cash flows

Cash flow adjustments, as we have seen in previous chapters, include those adjustments required to transform the accounting data into cash flow data. Typically, we add depreciation and amortization because they are non-cash subtractions from operating income after taxes. Capital expenditures have to be subtracted (or asset disposals have to be added) since these cash outflows (or cash inflows) do not appear on the income statement and thus are not deducted from (or added to) operating income. Finally, subtracting the increase in net working capital (or adding the decrease in net working capital) transforms the recognized accounting revenues and costs into cash revenues and costs. What we are getting is referred to as 'free cash flows', which means those cash flows that are available to equity and debt holders after consideration for taxes, capital expenditures and net working capital needs. The free cash flows calculation is therefore:

Revenues

– Costs	(including depreciation and amortization)
EBIT	(earnings before interests and taxes or operating profit)
$\times (1 - T_c)$	T_c = corporate tax rate
EBIAT	(earnings before interests and after taxes or net operating profit after taxes)

+ Depreciation and Amortization

± Change in net working capital

± Capital expenditures or Asset disposals

= Free cash flow

Notice that all financing items (in particular interest charges) are *not* deducted to calculate the free cash flows since financing is incorporated in the cost of capital.[3] Do not count these financing items twice!

An equivalent method of computing free cash flows (often referred as the components approach, while the previous method is called the profit and loss approach) deducts from the revenues all the cash

---

[3] We will review the different ways of treating the financing items when we present the different methods around the DCF approach later on in this chapter.

expenses (excluding depreciation and amortization) and adds back the tax shield provided by depreciation and amortization. The adjustments for capital expenditures and changes in net working capital remain the same than previously.

The free cash flow calculation, in this second approach, is therefore:

Revenues

– Cash operating costs   (excluding depreciation and amortization)

E B I T D A   (earnings before interests, taxes, depreciation and amortization)

$\times (1 - T_c)$ T_c = Corporate tax rate

E B I D A A T   (earnings before interests, depreciation, amortization and after taxes)

+ (depreciation and amortization) $\times T_c$ (Tax shield provided by depreciation and amortization)

± Change in net working capital

± Capital expenditures or Asset disposals

= Free cash flow

The P&L approach can be written as:

$$FCF = [R - C - D] (1 - T_c) + D - CAPEX - \Delta NWC \qquad (4)$$

The components approach, using the same symbols, can be written as:

$$FCF = [R - C] (1 - T_c) + T_c D - CAPEX - \Delta NWC \qquad (5)$$

It is easy to show that (4) and (5) are equivalent. (4) can be restated as:

$$FCF = (R - C) (1 - T_c) - D + T_c D + D - CAPEX - \Delta NWC$$

which is the same as (5) after having eliminated $-D$ and $+D$.

Table 5.2 shows, with a simple example, that the two methods of converting accounting statements to free cash flows are equivalent.

Table 5.2 Two equivalent methods of converting accounting statements to free cash flows

P&L approach		Components approach	
Revenues	1000	Revenues	1000
− Operating cost	600	− Cash operating costs	500
(including depreciation of 100)			
E B I T	400	E B I T D A	500
− Taxes (40%)	160	− Taxes (40%)	200
E B I A T	240	E B I D A A T	300
+ Depreciation	100	+ T_c × Depreciation	40
		(40% of 100)	
− Increase in NWC	80	− Increase in NWC	80
− Capital expenditures	120	− Capital expenditures	120
= Free cash flow	140	= Free cash flow	140

5.3.2 Terminal value

At the end of a forecasting horizon, we must make some estimate of the cash flow to be realized at that point or the value that lies in cash flows expected beyond the forecasting horizon. This estimate is called the terminal value. In many projects, the magnitude of this terminal value is suspect. It is not uncommon for terminal values to contribute 80% or more of the total value. It is therefore a critical parameter to assess. Remember your investment in real estate: your assumption of resale value (€180,000) was equivalent to €142,890 in present value, which represents more than 84% (€142,890/€169,863) of the total value of your apartment. And, to say the least, it is the parameter for which you feel the most uncomfortable!

Methods for approximating terminal values generally fall into two broad categories[4]:

The first one looks at terminal value in *liquidation* and applies essentially to assets with a finite life. This salvage value includes:

● The after-tax proceeds from the sale of assets (i.e. the cash inflow provided by the asset disposal plus or minus the tax credit or the tax payment produced by the capital loss (Salvage value < Book

[4] A good summary of the different methods is provided in 'Note on alternative methods for estimating terminal value', Harvard Business School N9–298–166.

value) or the capital gain (Salvage value > Book value) realized on the asset sale).
• The recovery, if any, of the net working capital.

The second category looks at terminal value from a *going concern* point of view and includes perpetuities and multiples.

A stable perpetuity is an infinite stream of constant cash flows and is equal to the cash flow divided by the discount rate. In other words, if, after the third year, you do not expect any increase of the rent you can charge on your apartment, its terminal value should have been €11,000/0.08 = €137,500 (instead of the €180,000 that we used in our previous calculation). Therefore, with this approach, the terminal value at period n would be given by the simple formula:

$$TV_n = \frac{CF_n}{k} \qquad (6)$$

A growing perpetuity is an infinite stream of cash flows growing at a rate g and the terminal value at period n, using this approach, is given by the following formula

$$TV_n = \frac{CF_n (1 + g)}{k - g} \qquad (7)$$

Notice that (6) is a special case of (7) when $g = 0$ (no growth of the cash flows).

If, after the third year, you expect the rent of your apartment to continue growing at an average rate of 5% per year, its terminal value at year would be given by

$$TV_3 = \frac{€11,000 (1 + 0.05)}{0.08 - 0.05} = €385,000$$

more than twice the €180,000 we used in our calculation.

This is telling you that the 5% growth for ever is probably too optimistic and your estimate relies on a much more realistic assumption of residual growth (in the area of 1.6%).

Be careful when using this growing perpetuity approach and remember the implications of fast growth *forever*. An asset cannot possibly and realistically grow faster than the average growth rate of the economy for a *very* long time!

Other ways to compute terminal values include multiple of book value and multiple of earnings. The basis of multiple of book value is to multiply the forecasted terminal-year book value of invested capital by an appropriate (usually the current) market value/book value ratio. To compute the terminal-year book value of invested capital, we use balance-sheet projections (terminal-year fixed assets and terminal-year net working capital).

The last method for establishing a terminal value is to multiply the forecasted terminal year profits (EBIAT, or EBIT or EBITDA) by an appropriate (usually the current one) earnings multiple. 'As a credibility check on any valuation calculation, it is often useful to try several approaches toward estimating a terminal value and hope for some convergence in the results. When results do not converge, it is important to understand the differing assumptions that produce the divergence. Judgement can then be applied to eliminate the resulting values that do not correctly reflect the assumptions of the decision maker'[5].

5.4 Business valuation: a review of different methods

5.4.1 Discounted cash flow valuation methods

The FCF–WACC method

The free cash flow–weighted average cost of capital method values the *whole* firm. Table 5.3 summarizes the main steps of the method and Table 5.4 provides an example.

This method takes a short cut. It accounts for the tax shield of debt in the discount rate (WACC) and therefore relies on several assumptions:

- Stable capital structure (D/E has to be constant, which means that if the market value of equity doubles, the amount of debt doubles too; if market value of the firm halves, debt halves too).
- Constant cost of debt and cost of equity.
- Constant tax rate.
- The firm is actually at its target capital structure and is able to pay the promised interest.
- The firm can use its interest tax shield in the year it occurs.

[5] 'Note on alternative methods for estimating terminal value', op. cit., p. 6.

Table 5.3 The cookbook for FCF–WACC

Step 1
Forecast relevant accounting statements

Step 2
Convert accounting statements to free cash flows using P & L approach or components approach

Step 3
Determine target capital structure (you might look at the capital structure of comparables. Firms in the same industry tend to have similar capital structures)

Step 4
Compute the weighted average cost of capital (WACC). We know how to calculate the WACC from Chapter 4

Step 5
Calculate the terminal value for the FCF using the most appropriate method. This can vary depending on the assumptions you make about what is going to happen at the end of the forecasted period. Will growth continue or slow down?

Step 6
Discount the free cash flows and the terminal value at the weighted average cost of capital

---

These assumptions impose severe limitations on the method which does not take account of the benefit provided by financial execution (since we use target capital structure weights), cannot easily incorporate some financial structures and accommodate subsidized debt and leads to important distortions for firms with high D/E ratios and debt with significant prospects of default.

When we move away from these assumptions, the modifications to WACC to make it work become very complicated (in particular the need to recompute the WACC for each period as capital structure changes) and the adjusted present value method is preferable[6].

The APV method

Still valuing the entire firm, APV uses the same FCF as the FCF–WACC method, but instead of adjusting the discount rate to account for the interest tax shield, it calculates this tax shield as a separate

---

[6] On the limitations and pitfalls of WACC and on the superiority of APV, see the excellent presentations by Timothy A. Luehrman, 'Using APV: a better tool for valuing operations', HBR May-June 1997 and 'What's it worth? A general manager's guide to valuation', HBR, May-June 1997.

component. In other words, APV separates the valuation exercise into one component associated with the project as if it were financed entirely with equity and another being made of the present value of all the effects associated with the project actual financing plan (PV of interest tax shield, value of subsidized debt, issue fees, guarantees, cost of financial distress . . .).

Table 5.4 Example of the FCF–WACC method

In January 2000, the company Bidder Ltd was considering the acquisition of Target Co., which would provide Bidder with an entry into an entirely new business. Target Co. generated sales of 1.5 million Euros in 1999. Bidder's assumptions about Target's future performance under its ownership were as follows:

Assumptions

Sales growth rate:	15% per year for the next 3 years
	After 3 years, no growth
Operating margin:	10% of sales
	(Note: this percentage assumes depreciation expense is deducted to determine operating profits)
Annual *incremental* investment in net working capital:	10% of *incremental* sales
Annual capital expenditures:	€35,000 in 2000
	Rising by €5,000 each year in 2001 and 2002
	Constant at €50,000 per year after 2002
Depreciation expense:	€20,000 in 2000
	Rising by €10,000 per year in 2001 and 2002
	Constant at €50,000 per year after 2002
Corporate tax rate:	35%
Target Co.'s equity beta (β_E):	1.50
Target Co.'s market-value debt ratio (D/V):	0.40 with $V = D+E$
Bidder, Inc.'s equity beta (β_E):	0.75
Bidder, Inc.'s market-value debt ratio (D/V):	0.25 with $V = D+E$
Risk-free rate:	5.70%
Equity market risk premium:	7.00%

In addition, it is known that Target Co. presently carries debt of €600,000, on which it pays annual interest equal to 7% of the balance outstanding at the beginning of the year. The debt will be reduced in increments of €100,000 at the end of each of the next two years (2000 and 2001). Thereafter, it was expected that the debt would remain constant at €400,000 and continue to cost 7% per annum.

Table 5.4   (*Continued*)

Steps 1 and 2
Using the assumptions given, free cash flows for Target Co. are estimated as follows:

	1990	2000	2001	2002	2003
Sales	1,500	1,725	1,984	2,281	2,281
Operating profit		172.5	198.4	228.1	228.1
– Taxes		(60.4)	(69.4)	(79.8)	(79.8)
EBIAT		112.1	129.0	148.3	148.3
+ Depreciation		20.0	30.0	40.0	50.0
– ΔNWC		(22.5)	(25.9)	(29.8)	0
– Cap. exp		(35.0)	(40.0)	(45.0)	(50.0)
Free cash flows		74.6	93.1	113.5	148.3

[all figures in thousands Euros].

Step 3
Target's Target capital structure is 40%

Step 4
Calculation of the weighted average cost of capital

Cost of Equity $k_E = r_F + \beta_E$ [equity market risk premium]
$\Rightarrow$ $k_E = 5.7\% + 1.5[7\%] = 16.2\%$

Cost of debt $k_D = 7\% \Rightarrow$ After-tax cost of debt $= (1 - t)\, k_D$
$\Rightarrow 0.65\,[7\%] = 4.55\%$

$\Rightarrow$ WACC $= 40\% \times 0.0455 + 60\% \times 0.162 = 11.54\%$

Step 5
Calculation of the terminal value using a no-growth perpetuity with the year 2003 free cash flow as the first year of that perpetuity

$$TV = € \frac{148.3}{0.1154} = 1285$$

Step 6
Discount the FCF and the terminal value at the WACC to get the value of the firm

$$V_F = \frac{74.6}{1.1154} + \frac{93.1}{(1.1154)^2} + \frac{113.5}{(1.1154)^3} + \frac{148.3 + 1285}{(1.1154)^4} = 1150$$

Step 7
Deduct the value of debt to get the value of the equity

$$V_F = V_E + V_D \Rightarrow V_E = V_F - V_D$$
$$\Rightarrow V_E = 1150 - 600 = 550$$

$$\text{APV} = \begin{array}{c} \text{FCF} \\ \text{discounted} \\ \text{at cost of} \\ \text{assets or} \\ \text{unlevered} \\ \text{cost of} \\ \text{equity} \end{array} + \begin{array}{c} \text{PV of tax} \\ \text{shield} \\ \text{discounted} \\ \text{at cost} \\ \text{of debt} \end{array} + \begin{array}{c} \text{PV of other} \\ \text{financing} \\ \text{side effects} \\ \text{(subsidies,} \\ \text{fees, etc.)} \end{array} - \begin{array}{c} \text{PV of the} \\ \text{cost of} \\ \text{financial} \\ \text{distress} \end{array}$$

So, in its formulation APV is valuation by parts and allows one to see how project value depends on the financing versus the assets themselves.

Table 5.5 summarizes the main steps of the method and Table 5.6 provides an example using the same data as in the example shown on Table 5.4.

The result is different mostly because the capital structure is changing through time. In addition, we have made some simplifying assumptions such as the debt beta being equal to zero. In fact, if the cost of debt for the company is 7%, while the risk-free rate is 5.7%

Table 5.5 The cookbook for APV

Step 1
Forecast relevant accounting statements and planned debt for an 'appropriate' period of time

Step 2
Convert accounting statements to free cash flows using P&L approach or components approach, and find value of interest tax shield in each year

- We know the tax shield in year i is $r \times D_i \times t_c$ where t_c is the tax rate

Step 3
Calculate terminal values for the FCF and the tax shield

Step 4
Discount the FCFs and the terminal value using K_c

- We know how to calculate K_c from Chapter 4

Step 5
Discount the tax shields and the tax shield TV using r

Step 6
Sum the present values you calculated in Steps 4 and 5. This is the adjusted present value of the firm

Table 5.5 (*Continued*)

Step 7

To get the value of equity, deduct the value of debt

Summary flow chart

Net present value of free cash flows

$$NPV = (CF_o) + \frac{FCF_1}{(1 + k_c)} + \frac{FCF_2}{(1 + k_c)^2} + \ldots + \frac{FCF_n + TVA}{(1 + k_c)^n}$$

Present value of tax shields

$$+ \frac{(t_c \times r \times D_1)}{(1 + r)} + \frac{(t_c \times r \times D_2)}{(1 + r)^2} + \ldots + \frac{(t_c \times r \times D_n) + TVTS}{(1 + r)^n}$$

Cost of capital

$$k_c = R_f + \beta_A (R_m - R_f)$$

Asset beta

$$\beta_A = \frac{E}{V} \beta_E$$

Symbol key

β_E	= Equity (levered) beta
β_A	= Asset (unlevered) beta
k_c	= Opportunity cost of capital
R_f	= Riskless rate of return
R_m	= Expected return on the market portfolio
r	= Interest rate on corporate debt
n	= Time period (n = 1, 2, 3, …)
D_n	= Euro amount of corporate debt outstanding in time period, n
E	= Market value of equity
V	= Total market value of the enterprise (sum of the market values of the debt and equity)
t_c	= Marginal corporate tax rate
CF_o	= Investment outlay at time 0
FCF_n	= Free cash flow expected in time period n
TVA	= Terminal value of assets
$TVTS$	= Terminal value of tax shields

and the equity market risk premium 7%, the implied beta of debt is 0.186 (7% = 5.7% + 0.186 × 7%)[7].

To reconcile the two methods, we will have to recompute the WACC each year, because the capital structure is changing every year and the cost of equity is also changing every year.

APV always works when a WACC approach works but it works also when WACC does not. APV is obviously not without some limitations: as

---

[7] If β_D is different from 0, then the relation between the asset beta and the equity beta is given by:

$$\beta_E = \left[\beta_A - \frac{D}{D + E} \beta_D \right] \bigg/ \frac{E}{D + E}$$

with all DCF methods, it assumes that the riskiness of future cash flows is such that it can be properly reflected in a stable discount rate. It is inaccurate when debt is risky because the interest tax shield is the promised rather than the expected interest tax shield. This is a problem which is shared by all DCF methods. The ability of the firm to default on its debt, i.e. the option to default, suggests that equity is a call option on the assets of the firm. If a firm is close to default (i.e. the firm value is less than the principal owed on the debt) much of the

Table 5.6 Example of the APV method

Steps 1 and 2
Free cash flows for Target Co. are the same as for the FCF–WACC method (see Table 5.4).

	2000	*2001*	*2002*	*2003*
Free cash flows	74.6	93.1	113.5	148.3

Interest expenses on Target's debt is expected to be as follows:

	1999	*2000*	*2001*	*2002*	*2003*
Principal	600	500	400	400	400
Interest	–	42	35	28	28
Tax shield	–	14.70	12.25	9.8	9.8

[all figures in thousand Euros]

Step 3
k_c is equal to $r_F + \beta_A$ [equity market risk premium]

with $\beta_A = \beta_E \dfrac{E}{D + E}$ (see Chapter 4)

$\beta_A = 1.50 \times 0.60 = 0.90$

$\Rightarrow k_c = 5.70\% + 0.90\,[7\%] = 12\%$

Therefore, the terminal value of the FCF, using a constant perpetuity is:

$\dfrac{148.3}{0.12} = 1235.8$

Step 4
Discount the free cash flows and the terminal value using 12% as a discount rate to get the value of the unlevered firm.

$$V_U = \frac{74.6}{1.12} + \frac{93.1}{(1.12)^2} + \frac{113.5}{(1.12)^3} + \frac{148.3 + 1235.8}{(1.12)^4} = 1101$$

Table 5.6 (*Continued*)

Step 5
Discount the tax shields and the terminal value of the tax shields using 7%, the cost of debt.

$$PV_{TS} = \frac{14.7}{1.07} + \frac{12.25}{(1.07)^2} + \frac{9.8}{(1.07)^3} + \frac{9.8 + 140^*}{(1.07)^4} = 147$$

*Assuming tax shields from 2003 onward are a no growth perpetuity, the terminal value of tax shields are 9.8/0.07 = 140.

Step 6
Sum the present value of the unlevered firm and the present value of the tax shields to get the value of the levered firm.

$$V_L = V_U + PV_{TS}$$
$$\Rightarrow V_L = 1101 + 147 = 1248$$

Step 7
Deduct the value of debt to get the value of equity.

$$V_E = V_F - V_D$$
$$\Rightarrow V_E = 1248 - 600 = 648$$

---

firm's equity value reflects option value[8] and the DCF techniques are more inaccurate. Finally another potential problem with APV is the possibility of a too sophisticated division of value into too many sub-components resulting in a useless complexity and a failure to check whether the pieces form a coherent unity. But despite these pitfalls, 'in its most basic form, which separates the value of the project from the value of its financing program, APV is easy to use. Ease of use, together with wider applicability and less scope for misuse than WACC makes it likely that APV eventually will become the DCF methodology of choice among practitioners'[9].

The capital cash flow (CCF) method, or compressed APV

The capital cash flow valuation method is a simplified version of APV (hence its alternative appellation, compressed APV). The difference between APV and compressed APV lies in the rate used to discount the tax shield of debt. So far, we have calculated the present value of the

---

[8] It is an out of the money option on the firm's assets.
[9] Note on adjusted present value, HBS, 9–293–092, p.7.

tax shields provided by debt as a separate item, using the cost of debt, k_d, as the discount rate. Compressed APV calls for discounting the tax shields of debt at the same rate as used to discount the value of the unlevered firm, namely k_c. Thus steps 3, 4 and 5 in Table 5.5 can be done altogether.

It is straightforward to show that the cash flows used in the Compressed APV method are:

> Compressed APV cash flows = Capital cash flows
> = Free cash flows of the firm
> + $t \times$ interests

where FCF are calculated as in the FCF–WACC or the APV method and t is the corporate tax rate.

The equity cash flow (ECF) method

Instead of valuing the entire firm and subtracting the value of the debt to find the equity value, this method values the equity directly by discounting equity cash flows, i.e. cash flows available to share-holders only (after payments to debtholders, interests and principal payments, have been deducted) at the cost of equity. It provides a way to value equity in highly levered transactions, such as LBOs (leveraged buyouts).

Table 5.7 shows the definition of equity cash flows, compared to the FCF. Table 5.8 compares equity cash flow to APV. Table 5.9 gives an

Table 5.7 Equity cash flow valuation

Equity cash flows are residual cash flows, to which equity holders are entitled. They are after-interest, after-tax, after-principal repayments.

EBIT	EBIT$(1-t)$
less: Interest	
Income before taxes	
less: Taxes	
Net income	
plus: Depreciation	plus: Depreciation
less: Capital expenditures	less: Capital expenditures
less: Increase in NWC	less: Increase in NWC
less: Principal repayments	
plus: New borrowing	
equals: Equity free cash flows	equals: FCF for the firm

Table 5.8 Comparing equity free cash flows to APV

Definitions:

FCF_{firm} = EBIT(1-t) + Depreciation – Capital expenditures – Increase in NWC

FCF_{debt} = Interest + Principal repayments – New debt proceeds

FCF_{equity} = Net income + Depreciation – Capital expenditures
– Increase in NWC – Principal repayments + New debt proceeds

Now add FCF_{debt} and FCF_{equity}:

$FCF_{debt} + FCF_{equity}$ = Interest + ~~Principal repayments~~ – ~~New debt proceeds~~
+ Net income + Depreciation – Capital expenditures
– Increase in NWC – ~~Principal repayments~~
+ ~~New debt proceeds~~

$FCF_{debt} + FCF_{equity}$ = Interest + Net income + Depreciation
– Capital expenditures – Increase in NWC

Note that Net income = (EBIT – Interest)(1–t)
= {EBIT(1–t) – Interest + Interest(t)}

Substituting:

$FCF_{debt} + FCF_{equity}$ = ~~Interest~~ + {EBIT(1-t) – ~~Interest~~ + Interest(t)}
+ Depreciation – Capital expenditures – Increase in NWC

Therefore:

$FCF_{debt} + FCF_{equity}$ =

EBIT(1-t)	+ Interest(t)
+ Depreciation – Capital expenditures	
– Increase in NWC	

This is simply FCFfirm

So:

$FCF_{debt} + FCF_{equity} = FCF_{firm} + Interest(t)$

| Debt-holders receive these | Equity-holders receive these | Cash from assets | Interest tax shield |

APV:

| Value of the debt | + | Value of the equity | = | Value of the firm |

Table 5.9 Example of the ECF method

---

*Using the assumptions given in Table 5.4, equity cash flows for Target Co. are estimated as follows:

	2000	2001	2002	2003
Sales	1,725	1,984	2,281	2,281
Operating profit (EBIT)	172.5	198.4	228.1	228.1
– Interests (7% of outstanding debt)	(42)	(35)	(28)	(28)
EBT (Earnings before taxes)	130.5	163.4	200.1	200.1
– Taxes (35%)	(45.7)	(57.2)	(70)	(70)
Net income	84.8	106.2	130.1	130.1
+ Depreciation	20	30	40	50
– ΔNWC	(22.5)	(25.9)	(29.8)	–
– Cap. exp.	(35)	(40)	(45)	(50)
– Principal repayments	(100)	(100)	–	–
Equity cash flows	(52.7)	(29.7)	96.3	130.1

[all figures in thousands Euros]

Cost of equity (see Table 5.4) = 16.2%.

Terminal value, using a no-growth perpetuity with the year 2003 equity cash flow as the first year of that perpetuity.

$$TV = \frac{130.1}{0.162} = 803.1$$

Discount the ECF and the terminal value at the cost of equity to get the value of the equity:

$$V_E = \frac{(52.7)}{(1.162)} + \frac{(29.7)}{(1.162)^2} + \frac{96.3}{(1.162)^3} + \frac{130.1 + 803.1}{(1.162)^4} = 506$$

---

example of the method, using the same data as the example shown in Table 5.4.

Again, due to some restrictive assumptions described earlier, it is difficult to compare the results provided by the various methods.

In addition to the common limitations attached to all DCF methods, the equity cash flow methodology is biased essentially because it ignores the equity holders' option to walk away from an insolvent firm, even if it is in their best interests to do so. Therefore this approach 'will be most useful when leverage is high, but not too high, that is when debt is clearly risky, but the firm is clearly solvent. For firms within this range, the equity cash flow methodology is a good way to obtain a lower bound for the value of the equity'[10].

---

[10] 'Note on valuing equity cash flows', Harvard Business School, 9–295–085, p. 9.

Table 5.10 summarizes the key characteristics and differences of the three DCF methods.

5.4.2 Methods based on comparables

Comparable companies

The basic idea is to identify a set of comparable firms. A firm is comparable if it is identical in every way that affects cash flows and discount rates. For this set of comparables, multiples of enterprise values relative to sales, earnings (EBITDA or EBIT) and cash flows and multiples of equity values relative to net profit are derived. When relevant ranges of multiples for the comparable companies have been determined, the method simply calculates imputed total firm values, or equity firm values, by applying actual and forecasted sales, EBITDA, EBIT and net profit of the company which is evaluated to the multiples derived from the analysis of the comparable companies. An example of such a calculation by Credit Suisse First Boston in its Fairness Opinion Relating to the valuation of CarnaudMetalbox[11] is shown in Table 5.11.

The obvious advantages of the method is that it is very intuitive, straightforward and simple to implement. The caveat is to make sure that comparables are in fact really comparable, not only in terms of activities and businesses but also in terms of capital structure, leverage, future growth and dividend payout. We know, for example, that price–earning ratios are sensitive to leverage. So when using a comparable company, we have to check that it has a comparable leverage or adjust PER for leverage.

Comparable transactions

Comparable transactions or premium-paid analyses look at the purchase prices and multiples paid in selected prior transactions, usually in the same industry. By getting, as before, a range of multiples for comparable acquired companies and a range of premia paid in these similar transactions and by applying these multiples and premia to the company we are valuing, we obtain a range of values.

Table 5.12 shows the evaluation of CarnaudMetalbox by Credit Suisse First Boston using this approach.

Valuation using multiples is technically simple, it does not explicitly incorporate assumptions about the business, but knowing which type of multiple to use and identifying the correct comparables are not easy

[11] Credit-Suisse-First-Boston Fairness Opinion Relating to Crown Cork and Seal Company INC's offer to purchase CarnaudMetalbox for FF225 per share? Nov. 14, 1995.

Table 5.10 Key characteristics of the three DCF methods

	FCF–WACC	Equity cash flow	Adjusted present value (APV)
Cash flow definition	FCF = EBIT $(1-t)$ + Depr $-$ Cap Ex $- \Delta$ NWC	ECF = NI + Depr $-$ Cap Ex $- \Delta$NWC $-$ Principal Repayments $+$ New Borrowings	Each component has separate cash flow line: 1 FCF (same as in WACC method) used to find the value of the *unlevered* firm. 2 Interest Tax Shields (interest × tax rate) to find the value of leverage 3 Other financing side effects. To use the *Compressed APV* format, add the FCF to the Interest Tax Shields
Estimate *firm* value or *equity* value?	Firm value. Subtract value of debt to get equity value.	Equity value. Add value of debt to get firm value.	Firm value. Subtract value of debt to get equity value
Where are the interest tax shields?	Accounted for in the discount rate (WACC incorporates a $(1-t)$ term)	In the cash flows (starting with NI insures that we end up with the after-tax cost of debt)	In the cash flows, but evaluated as a separate component.
Which discount rate?	WACC	K_e (levered cost of equity).	Depends on the component. K_U for value of the unlevered firm; K_D for the value of the interest tax shields. For *Compressed APV*, discount all at K_U
Update discount rate with leverage changes?	Yes, but if leverage changes, WACC is not the most appropriate method	Yes. K_e is very sensitive to leverage changes	No. K_U is invariant to leverage changes.
When to use?	When debt is a fixed percentage of capital structure, and there are *no* other financing side-effects	ECF can effectively be used in changing leverage situations when the debt is not too risky. ECF is the only method which evaluates one layer of the capital structure directly.	When debt is fixed in level, rather than a % of firm value. Changing leverage situations; complex financing side effect calculations. APV works when other (simpler) DCF techniques do, and it also works in some cases where other DCF techniques do not.

Table 5.11 Comparable company analysis

CS First Boston reviewed and compared certain actual and forecasted financial and operating information of the Metal Packaging and Plastic Packaging businesses of CarnaudMetalbox with comparable information of the following publicly traded companies in the packaging industry: Pechiney International SA, Schmalbach-Lubeca AG, Ball Corporation, US Can Corp., The West Company, Inc., Kerr Group, Inc. and Continental Can Co., Inc. (the 'Packaging Comparable Companies'). In addition, CS First Boston reviewed and compared certain actual and forecasted financial and operating information of the engineering and other business of CarnaudMetalbox with comparable information of the following publicly traded companies in the packaging machinery industry: Sasib S.p.A and APV Plc (the 'Engineering Comparable Companies' and, together with the Packaging Comparable Companies, the 'Comparable Companies'). CS First Boston selected these companies based on their activity in businesses comparable to the Crown businesses and CarnaudMetalbox businesses. CS First Boston derived multiples of enterprise values relative to estimated sales, EBITDA, and earnings before interest and taxes ('EBIT') for the 1994 and 1995 calendar years. In addition, CS First Boston derived multiples of equity values relative to estimated net income for the 1994 and 1995 calendar years. CS First Boston determined that the relevant ranges of multiples for the Comparable Companies were: (1) sales: 0.5× to 1.3×; (2) EBITDA: 4.0× to 6.3×; (3) EBIT: 7.0× to 9.4×; and (4) net income: 9.7× to 14.2×. CS First Boston then calculated imputed enterprise values of CarnaudMetalbox by applying forecasted sales, EBITDA, EBIT and net income for CarnaudMetalbox for the fiscal year 1995 to the multiples derived from its analysis of the Comparable Companies. This analysis resulted in an enterprise valuation reference range for the Metal Packaging business. Plastic Packaging business, and engineering and other business of CarnaudMetalbox of approximately FF 13,000 million – FF 15,000 million, FF 3,900 million – FF 4,100 million and FF 500 million – FF 600 million, respectively.

All forecasted sales, EBITDA, EBIT and net income multiples for the Comparable Companies were based on information contained in equity research reports. The enterprise values and equity values of the Comparable Companies used in the foregoing analyses were based on closing stock prices as of 3 May 1995. CS First Boston also reviewed and compared certain actual and forecasted financial and operating information of the Crown businesses with comparable information of the Packaging Comparable Companies. All financial estimates for Crown and Carnaud-Metalbox for the 1995 financial year were based on certain operating and financial forecasts provided by Crown.

---

tasks. This approach should be viewed, in any case, as an approximation of the value of the asset or company and as complementary information to the DCF results.

Over the past years, DCF approaches have been widely criticized. 'Although the NPV rule is relatively easy to apply, it is built on faulty assumptions. It assumes one of two things: either that the investment is reversible (in other words, that it can somehow be undone and the expenditures recovered should market conditions turn out to be worse than anticipated); or that, if the investment is irreversible, it is

Table 5.12 Comparable acquisition analysis

Using publicly available information, CS First Boston analysed the purchase prices and multiples paid in the following transactions in the packaging industry: the acquisition of Lawson Mardon Group Ltd. by Alusuisse Lonza Holding AG; the acquisition of Van Dorn Company by Crown; the acquisition of Heekin Can. Inc. by Ball Corporation; the acquisition of Continental Can Europe, Inc. by VIAG AG; the acquisition of Continental Can Canada Inc. by Crown; the acquisition of Triangle Industries, Inc. by Pechiney International SA; the acquisition of Zeller Plastik Group GmbH by CarnaudMetalbox; the acquisition of Impetus Packaging, Ltd. by VIAG AG; the acquisition of CONSTAR International Inc. by Crown; and the acquisition of DRG Medical Packaging Mount Holly by Bowater Inc. CS First Boston selected these acquisitions based on the activity of the acquired companies in businesses comparable to that of Crown and CarnaudMetalbox. CS First Boston calculated the adjusted purchase price (purchase price plus total assumed debt less assumed cash) as a multiple of sales, EBITDA and EBIT of each acquired company for the latest available 12 month period immediately preceding the announcement of the acquisition of such company and calculated the purchase price as a multiple of the net income of each acquired company for such period. CS First Boston determined that the relevant range of multiples for the comparable acquired metal packaging companies were: (1) sales: $0.4\times$ to $1.5\times$; (2) EBITDA: $5.8\times$ to $10.6\times$; (3) EBIT: $7.8\times$ to $16.9\times$; and (4) net income: $12.2\times$ to $21.0\times$. CS First Boston determined that relevant range of multiples for the comparable acquired plastic packaging companies were: (1) sales: $0.5\times$ to $1.5\times$; (2) EBITDA: $5.1\times$ to $9.5\times$; (3) EBIT: $6.8\times$ to $14.8\times$; and (4) net income: $11.4\times$ to $32.4\times$. CS First Boston then calculated imputed enterprise values of CarnaudMetalbox by applying forecasted sales, EBITDA, EBIT and net income for CarnaudMetalbox for fiscal year 1995 to the multiples derived from its analyses of the acquired companies. This analysis resulted in an enterprise valuation reference range for CarnaudMetalbox's Metal Packaging business and Plastic Packaging business of approximately FF 18,000 million–FF 22,000 million and FF 5,000 million – FF 6,000 million, respectively. CS First Boston also calculated imputed enterprise values of Crown by applying forecasted sales, EBITDA, EBIT and net income for Crown for the fiscal year 1995 to the multiples derived from its analysis of the acquired companies.

---

a now-or-never proposition (if the company does not make the investment now, it will lose the opportunity forever)[12]. 'Unfortunately, the financial tool most widely relied on to estimate the value of strategy – DCF valuation – assumes that we will follow a pre-determined plan, regardless of how events unfold. A better approach to valuation would incorporate both the uncertainty inherent in business and the active decision making required for a strategy to succeed . . . In financial terms, a business strategy is much like a series of options than a series of static cash flows'[13]. We will not review, in this book, the real option approach to valuation, since it has not yet received many practical applications.

[12] Avinash K. Dixit and Robert S. Pindyck, 'The options approach to capital investment', HBR, May–June, 1995, p. 106.

5.5 Discounted cash flow methods and economic value added (EVA)

As we have seen, at the beginning of this chapter, in the investment techniques, NPV is the difference between the present value of expected cash flows and the present value of the initial investment, which can be written as:

$$NPV = \frac{FCF_1}{(1 + WACC)} + \frac{FCF_2}{(1 + WACC)^2} + \ldots + \frac{FCF_n}{(1 + WACC)^n} - I_o$$

> where   *FCF*   stands for the free cash flows of each year,
>   *WACC* stands for the weighted average cost of capital,
> and I_O stands for the initial invested capital.

If we assume a steady-state situation, with no growth, in which depreciation is equal to capital expenditures and changes in working capital are equal to zero, then the free cash flows are equal to the net operating profit after taxes (NOPAT) or, as we have called it on several occasions, the earnings before interests and after taxes (EBIAT).

Using the formula of a constant perpetuity (section 5.3 of this chapter), we can write NPV as:

$$NPV = \frac{EBIAT}{WACC} - I_o = \frac{EBIT\,(1\text{-}t)}{WACC} - I_o$$

or

$$NPV = EBIT\,(1\text{-}t) - WACC \times I_o$$

Which is exactly the definition of the economic value added (see Chapter 4). This means that EVA can be viewed as a static measure, incorporating the key features of DCF analysis, in a steady-state situation of no growth.

[13] Timothy A. Luehrman, 'Strategy as a portfolio of real options', HBR, September–October 1998, pp. 89–90. See also from the same author 'Investment opportunities as real options: getting started on the numbers', HBR, July–August, 1998, an excellent article bridging the gap between the practicalities of real-world-capital projects and the higher mathematics associated with formal option pricing theory.

5.6 Value creation and value drivers

As we have said several times, the economic value of a business depends on its ability to generate future cash flows. A good measure of a business value is therefore the present value of the expected stream of cash flows. The task of management is to increase these expected cash flows to create value. The definition of free cash flows allows us to understand how management can increase these expected cash flows and create value. It will do it

1 by acting on sales (rate of growth of sales and duration of the sales growth);
2 by maximizing the operating margin;
3 by managing taxes so as to reduce, in obviously a complete legal way, the effective tax rate;
4 by minimizing the investment in net working capital;
5 and by rationalizing the investment in fixed capital.

Table 5.13 summarizes some very general action that management can take to increase the stream of cash flows generated by the firm.

Table 5.13   Value drivers

Promote growth
● Increase business with current customers
● Pursue high growth segments within broader markets
● Expand global presence
● Pursue complementary alliances and acquisitions

Improve margins
● Focus on restructuring, efficiency, productivity and cost control

Lower working capital
● Increase inventory turns
● Focus on collection processes
● Get best conditions from suppliers

Optimize asset utilization
● Lower capital expenditures
● Improve turnover ratios

Reduce effective taxes
● Lower tax rates, by using all tax benefits provided by law
● Use international status to benefit from best tax provisions

Optimize cost of capital
● Reduce cost of various financing means
● Do not deviate from optimal capital structure

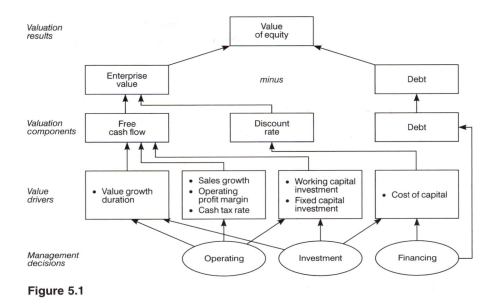

Valuation results

Valuation components

Value drivers

Management decisions

Figure 5.1

These cash flows being then discounted at the cost of capital to give the value of the firm, the last way to increase the enterprise value is to minimize the cost of capital.

Figure 5.1 shows the links between management decisions, value drivers and valuation results.

By identifying and understanding the levers that drive a company's value in the long term, we can expect more focused behaviour by managers, better strategic planning, more rational resource allocation and better designed incentive compensation systems.

The action steps towards building a culture of concern for value creation within the organization are the following:

- Develop a common understanding among managers of what drives value in the company.
- Establish decision guidelines, rules and processes which focus management attention on the goal of creating value.
- Implement management evaluation and incentive systems that encourage managers to make value-creating decisions.

Because cash flow philosophy avoids accounting distortions and reveals the true economic value of the firm, because long-term time horizon discourages managing for short-term results and because time value of money and risk are properly reflected in the methodology, discounted cash flow and value-based management are superior to traditional accounting approaches and performance measures.

6

Shareholder value: a European perspective

There has been a fast changing landscape in Europe and an increasing trend for European managers to focus on shareholder value. While this increased focus on shareholder value will not remove all the barriers and problems in the European context, it will lead to better utilization of capital from pension funds, and other investors, institutional or personal. As the US model has illustrated in the 1990s, the focus on shareholder value increases the size of the pie, which could then be divided between equity stockholders, senior managers, workers and other stakeholders. Despite the short-term dislocations caused by some restructuring operations such as demergers, the long-term benefits to the remaining employees outweigh the social costs.

European restructuring has been delayed by misguided patriotism with governments determined to pursue nationalistic goals.[1] Over the years, they forgot that ownership nationality is often irrelevant to the creation of wealth. An efficient foreign-owned subsidiary does more for the economy than a sick independent nationally subsidized champion. As Schumpeter taught us, the essence of capitalism revolves around 'creative destruction', and European countries should allow companies to restructure or disappear. He also believed that economic progress in a capitalist society means turmoil. The Euro will lead to increased competition throughout Europe as prices become more transparent. The introduction of the Euro and the realization by governments, in most European countries, that they are sitting on a pension bomb with their ageing populations will leave them no choice but to finally allow this wave of deregulation, restructuring and equity culture to continue. Furthermore, companies that are pressured by shareholders to deliver higher returns, will in turn push local governments to lighten the tax load and remove labour and other restrictions. Nevertheless, the

We wish to thank Sam Abboud, Thomas Fetzer, Adrian Fopp and Sotiris Lyritzis for their contribution to parts of this chapter.

[1] 'The National Factor', Peter Martin, *Financial Times*, 31 August 1999, p. 12.

institutional rigidities and barriers will continue to pose challenges slowing down the restructuring process.

We first briefly outline some of the key drivers and barriers to change in the European context and then discuss in more detail three main strategic moves towards delivering shareholder value: mergers and acquisitions, spinoffs, demergers and carve-outs and finally share repurchases.

6.1 The main drivers of change in Europe towards shareholder value

6.1.1 The development of equity markets in Europe and the emergence of an equity culture

The traditional underdevelopment of equity markets in Continental Europe has been one of the main obstacles to the development of shareholder value. The market capitalization as a percentage of GDP is low in Continental Europe compared with Anglo American figures, particularly in countries such as France, Germany, Italy and Spain as Figure 6.1. shows. Table 6.1 compares Euroland (the eleven countries which have adopted the Euro as a common currency) with the USA and Japan.

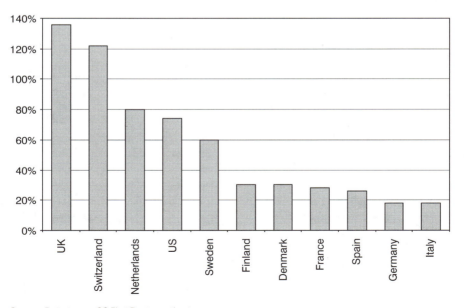

Source: Datastream, CS First Boston estimates

Figure 6.1 Market capitalization as a percentage of GDP
Source: Datastream, CS First Boston estimates

Table 6.1   Comparison of capitalization

	Euroland	US	Japan
Population (millions)	292	268	120
GDP	$6.3 trillion	$8.1 trillion	$4.2 trillion
Equity market cap.	$2.1 trillion	$6.9 trillion	$3.7 trillion
Number of listed companies	2,800	8,600	1,865

Source: Wall Street Journal Europe, 1/4/99: For Japan: World Exchange Fact Book: 1998.

Several factors are contributing to the expansion of stock markets in Europe.

- The *privatization of major financial and industrial sectors* leads to a higher number of stocks listed and an improved liquidity of the markets. Stock ownership by the state or state owned institutions, large banks and 'core strategic' corporate shareholders which has been traditionally high in France, Germany and Italy is declining everywhere, even if it remains significant as shown in Table 6.2, and market forces are increasingly putting pressure on corporate management to maximize shareholder value.

Table 6.2   Equity ownership pattern of listed companies

Country	Individuals and non-profit organizations	Pension and other funds Insurance companies	Banks, government, other	Corporations	Foreign	Total
Australia	19%	35%	4%	11%	31%	100%
Canada	15%	38%	8%	14%	25%	100%
France	23%	12%	14%	14%	37%	100%
Germany	17%	15%	17%	39%	12%	100%
Italy	16%	13%	43%	18%	10%	100%
Japan	20%	21%	23%	28%	8%	100%
Netherlands	14%	21%	1%	23%	41%	100%
Sweden	23%	30%	8%	9%	30%	100%
UK	19%	58%	5%	2%	16%	100%
US	51%	41%	3%	0%	5%	100%

Source: Spencer Stuart, *A Glance at Corporate Governance Around the World.*

- *The growing popularity of stock-options and employee shareholding schemes* will play a significant role in establishing an 'equity culture' in Continental Europe.[2]
- *The rise of pension funds in Europe* will be a major force in developing the depth, volume and efficiency of European stock markets. 'Following the example of the UK which has a well developed pension fund system, continental stock markets should benefit from the expansion of pension fund assets . . . Such a trend will undoubtedly promote an equity culture in Europe and strengthen the position of individual shareholders'.[3] The demographic forces will put tremendous pressure on pension funds for improved performance. Table 6.3 shows the European pension fund assets current allocation.

Some forecasts suggest that total Euro-zone equity market capitalization (including the UK) could double by 2005. Some others estimate that there will be $13 trillion of cash inflows into European equity by 2010.[4]

Table 6.3 Pension fund assets currently in equities

	Percentage invested in equities	*Current allocation of equity investments*	
		Domestic	*Int'l*
Belgium	30%	57%	43%
Finland	8%	88%	13%
Germany	9%	67%	33%
Ireland	58%	40%	60%
Italy	1%	100%	0%
Netherlands	29%	38%	62%
Portugal	8%	75%	25%
Spain	5%	100%	0%
Denmark	22%	77%	23%
Sweden	28%	71%	29%
Switzerland	14%	79%	21%
UK	77%	70%	30%

Sources: *Euromoney*, 'Investment Banking, The gold-diggers of Europe 1999', 9/10/98, p. 48.

[2] France joins the stakeholder revolution, *Financial Times*, 21 May 1999, p. 25.
[3] *Shareholder value in Europe*, CS First Boston, 18 April 1996, p. 10.
[4] 'Investment banking, the gold-diggers of Europe 1999', *Euromoney*, September 1998, p. 48.

- *Economic value added and other value based management tools* are becoming more and more common for European companies, pushing European executives to align corporate objectives and decision making with shareholders' interests.

6.1.2 The growing internationalization of stock markets and the increasing share of US ownership

The globalization of capital markets has led US institutional investors to diversify internationally. 'The increasing share of US ownership is likely to be a positive catalyst for European Corporate management to focus more on shareholder value.'[5]

It has, in any case, led to some strong conflicts between European business practices and the investment philosophy of US investors, particularly US pension funds, as illustrated by the Alcatel loss of 70 billion French Francs in a few hours on 17 September 1998.[6]

6.2 The remaining barriers to shareholder value focus in Europe

6.2.1 Lack of information transparency

New investors are demanding changes in the European context. Unlike traditional banks with long established relationships over generations with companies, the new capital requires more disclosure of financial information. The historic information asymmetry between managers and outside investors has led to poor investment decisions and misallocation of capital to under-performing companies. Despite the recent efforts by several European companies to disclose more information, most companies with the exception of those in the UK are still far behind US public companies. The European Economic Community is working towards creating common standards within the continent, but it will take years before such a standard is implemented. Table 6.4 shows major differences between accounting policies in some European countries and between these European countries and the US.

- Many countries allow assets to be written up to market value, assessed value, or replacement cost. This practice can increase

---

[5] Shareholder value in Europe, *op. cit.*
[6] US Pension Funds Unnerve French, *International Herald Tribune*, 3 October, 1998.

Table 6.4 Sample accounting practices

Practice	France	Germany	Italy	UK	USA
Consolidation of parent and subsidiary account required?	Yes, when listed on the stock exchange	Yes	Only if required by the securities regulatory agency	Yes	Yes
Transfers to/from Reserves are easily traceable?	Yes	Large contingent liabilities may be undisclosed	Varies, few disclosures and limited prior data restrict tracing	Yes	Yes
Periodic asset revaluation allowed?	Write-up to appraised value allowed	No, fixed assets carried at cost	Yes, according to an index and government decree	Fixed assets may be carried at market value	No
Reported financial statements any differ from tax accounts?	Yes, deferred tax effects disclosed in footnotes	Seldom, due to relatively minor timing issues	Minor differences due to timing issues	Yes, mainly due to depreciation and timing differences	Yes
Capitalization of financial leases required?	Not permitted, rental commitments disclosed in notes	No requirement in the civil code	No requirement in the civil code	Yes	Yes
Purchased goodwill amortization period	Immediately against reserves up to a maximum of 5 years	Amortized up to 15 years for taxes 1 to 4 years in annual reports	Immediately against reserves	Immediately against reserves up to useful economic life	40 years
Independent third-party audit?	Yes	Yes	Yes	Yes	Yes

Source: *Valuation, Measuring and Managing the Value of Companies*, Tom Copeland, Tim Koller and Jack Nurrin, 2nd edition, pp. 397–400.

and easily distort cross-company estimates of the return on capital employed.

- The treatment of goodwill varies widely between different countries. It may or may not be a tax deductible expense. It may be written off immediately against reserves or it may be written off over a period as long as 40 years. Comparisons of ROCE across companies can be significantly distorted by the treatment of goodwill.
- In some countries, e.g. Germany, the annual report to the shareholders and the tax books use the same accounting standards.
- Reserves are often used as non-cash write-offs of anticipated long-term expenses such as pensions, reorganization, maintenance and other costs.

6.2.2 Significant agency costs between managers and shareholders

The lack of proper disclosure also leads to significant agency costs between the owners and the managers. In the 1970s and 1980s, executives throughout Europe engaged in numerous unrelated acquisitions, which are currently being divested, as discussed later in the Spin-off section. With no equity at stake in the corporations they are running, managers had no direct financial incentives to improve performance. Furthermore, the old fixed compensation system over-compensated low and medium performers and grossly under-compensated high performers. The most direct way to reduce agency problems is through high-powered incentive schemes, by tying CEO and other senior executives' pay closely to shareholder value creation. This is changing with the introduction of stock options, EVA and other performance-based compensation throughout Europe. For the same value transfer to the executive, options have greater pay-to-performance sensitivity than stock; and out-of-the-money options have greater sensitivities than at-the-money options.[7] The increased level of private equity investments and cross-border mergers and acquisitions are also driving the export of US style compensation systems to Europe. In turn, equity-linked incentive plans should lead to better alignment of senior management and shareholders' interests, reducing agency costs in major public corporations. It will be more difficult to establish appropriate incentive and compensation plans for senior managers in the case of small or private family-owned business such as the German Mittelstand, which accounts for about 50% of all private sector, 40% of

[7] Brian Hall, 'The pay to performance incentives of executive stock options', NBER 6674, August 1998.

total investment, and two-thirds of all private sector employment.[8] This is due to the following reasons:

- No or thinly traded common stock, which makes it harder to measure and reward superior management performance.
- Reluctance of family shareholders to give managers an equity stake in the business.
- Family shareholders may be more interested in maximizing liquidity and short-term cash flow rather than long-term value.

The growth of the high yield market will also reduce agency costs in two ways. First, the 'sword of debt' and restrictive covenants will force managers to be more careful in managing their cash flow. High leverage affects executive incentives by making default and even bankruptcy a probable result of poor corporate performance. There is compelling evidence that managers often lose their jobs, and suffer serious career and reputation damage, when their companies default on their debt or file for bankruptcy.[9] Moreover, a high yield market will facilitate hostile takeover of companies with under-performing management teams. It might take years before the market for corporate control develops, as cross-holding and bank ownership blocks are liquidated throughout Europe. For example, since the Second World War, there have been very few hostile public takeover bids in Germany. Nevertheless, the availability of huge pool of high yield capital will pose an increasing threat to weak executives in Europe.

6.2.3 Strong labour market rigidities

European workers have posed major barriers in the past to the efficient use of capital. The strong power of the unions in Germany, France and other countries has prevented senior management from implementing cost savings measures. Historically, European politicians and labour unions have been very hostile to layoffs and plant closures, an essential tool for US-style restructuring.[10] Employee power across Europe is outlined in Table 6.5.

Europe's rigid labour markets have contributed to the high unemployment rate of more than 11% (compared with 4% in the USA), despite the low interest rate environment in Europe. Labour laws and regulation need to change throughout Europe to allow managers

[8] Thomas McGraw, *Creating Modern Capitalism*, p. 180.
[9] Gilson S. and M. Vetsuypens, 'Creating pay-for-performance in financially troubled companies', *Journal of Applied Corporate Finance*, Winter 1994, pp. 81–92.
[10] 'US buyout firms search for deals in Europe', *The Wall Street Journal*, 30 December 1998, p. A4.

Table 6.5 Employee power across Europe

Germany	<ul><li>Employees have up to 50% of seats on supervisory board</li><li>Employees have decision-sharing power in personnel and social matters</li></ul>
Netherlands	<ul><li>The workers council has a right to information and consultation, and the right to grant or withhold approval of certain decisions</li><li>Veto on appointment of directors</li></ul>
Belgium	<ul><li>CEO must provide the workers council with detailed data on internal operations</li><li>Workers council gives opinion and suggestions in some areas</li></ul>
France	<ul><li>Two employee representatives may attend board meetings but have no voting right</li></ul>
UK	<ul><li>Management has no obligation to consult or involve employees in decision making</li></ul>
Denmark	<ul><li>Employees have a statutory right to co-determination</li></ul>

Source: McKinsey Global Institute, Service Sector Productivity, 1992.

greater flexibility in the face of competition from US and Asian companies.

Labour mobility is naturally more restricted in Europe than in the US. Despite the dismantling of national borders, workers in Europe still face language and cultural barriers that prevent them from taking advantage of opportunities in other countries or regions.

6.2.4 Harsh bankruptcy laws

Besides the reluctance to lay off workers, several large European corporations have also been unwilling to increase their debt levels. This risk aversion to leverage could be partially explained by the grim prospects for in-court restructuring and harsh bankruptcy laws in most European countries. For example, German laws make it very difficult to complete an out-of-court restructuring by imposing civil and criminal liabilities on the management team if it does not file for bankruptcy in time. In-court restructuring in Germany almost always results in liquidation. In France, the Bankruptcy Law passed in 1985 was intended to save jobs by keeping troubled companies alive, but it has not reached its objectives and over 90% of in-court cases continue to end up in liquidation. This is in sharp contrast to the US where 92% of distressed firms first attempt to restructure out of court, and only 53% of restructuring attempts end in Chapter 11.[11] The UK Insolvency Act of 1986 places more emphasis on protecting the rights of creditors. Since 1987, the majority of distressed cases in the UK have ended in liquidation. In bankruptcies, courts in the UK may require the directors to make contribution to the company assets by imposing personal liabilities.[12] Managers in the UK are loath to seek an insolvency filing, because it will result not only in the termination of employment, but often in painful personal disgrace. Finally, unlike managers in the US who benefit from automatic stay and have to come up with their own restructuring plan during a Chapter 11 filing, managers in Europe lose control of the reorganization process during bankruptcy and are often replaced immediately. As a result of all these bankruptcy laws and cultural issues, European managers have developed an ingrained fear of debt and strong solvency orientation leading to overall lower leverage levels and less than optimal capital structures.

6.2.5 Unfavourable tax environment

As discussed later in both the Spin-off and Share repurchase sections, tax regulations in the various European countries have led managers to poor use of equity capital, leading to inefficient capital structures. For example, French law taxed proceeds from share buybacks at the higher marginal income tax rate which was recently reduced to the lower capital gain rate. Similarly, tax laws and other restrictions in Germany made it virtually impossible to implement a tax-free spin-off until recently. Over the past two years, there have been several changes in the tax codes in various European countries which will allow for more share repurchase programmes and other shareholder oriented corporate financial policies. For example, tax legislation was introduced in Spain to give a new impetus to investments in non-quoted companies.

6.3 Mergers and acquisitions (M&A) in Europe

The 1990s saw an unprecedented growth in M&A activity in Europe, with the transactions at the end of the decade being three-and-a-half times as high as those at the beginning of the decade as shown in Figure 6.2.

---

[11] Gilson, S. and others, 'Troubled debt restructuring: an empirical study of private reorganization of firms in default', *Journal of Financial Economics*, **26** (1990), pp. 315–353.
[12] Note on International Comparisons Concerning Troubled Companies, HBS 9.293.090

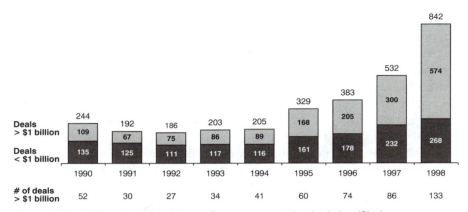

Figure 6.2 M&A volume involving a European party by deal size ($bn)
Source: Securities Data Company, J.P. Morgan, 'Global M&A Review, January 1999

The most active sectors have been the financial industry (with a total volume of $181 billion) and utilities (with $166 billion) as indicated in Figure 6.3.

The dominant deals have been ones where European companies bought non-European targets. Major transactions, to mention a few of them, were BP/Amoco, Daimler/Chrysler and Deutsche Bank/Bankers Trust. The rationale behind the transactions has been global

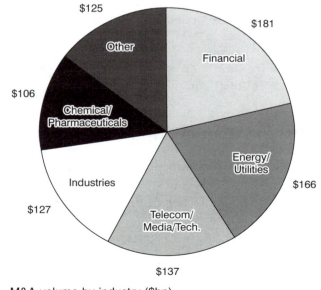

Figure 6.3 M&A volume by industry ($bn)
Source: J.P. Morgan, January 1999

positioning, since increasingly integrated international markets are calling for firms expanding their global reach.

Although smaller in overall deal size, there has been a significant activity by non-European acquirers buying European firms, such as Universal Studios/Polygram (USA/Netherlands), or Texas Utilities/ Energy Group (USA/UK). The second largest category has been intra-European deals, for which the progress of the Eurozone has accelerated the process. Notable transactions have included Astra/ Zeneca (Sweden/UK), Hoescht/Rhone-Poulenc (Germany/France), Total/Petrofina (France/Belgium) and Vodaphone/Mannesmann (UK/Germany).

Domestic European M&A, although large as a category, have exhibited the slowest growth. This probably indicates that a great deal of domestic consolidation has already taken place and that management teams are now focusing on international expansion. Table 6.6 lists the recent biggest deals in Europe.

Table 6.6   M&A top ten deals (1 January to 19 June 2000)

Target	Acquirer	Value of deal ($m)
SmithKline Beecham (UK)	Glaxo Wellcome (UK)	78,384.5
Orange (Mannesmann) (UK)	France Telecom (France)	45,967.1
Allied Zurich (UK)	Zurich Allied (Switzerland)	19,399.1
Seat Paglne Gialle (Italy)	Tln.lt (Italy)	18,694.3
Norwich Union (UK)	CGU (UK)	11,858.3
Credit Commercial de France (France)	HSBC Holdings (UK)	11,223.0
Mannesmann Atecs (Germany)	Investor Group (Germany)	9,394.1
Telia AB (Sweden)	Investors (Unknown)	8,897.0
AOL Europe, AOL Australia (Germany)	America Online (US)	8,250.0
Dordtsche Petroleum (Netherlands)	Investor Group (Netherlands)	8,125.2

Source: Thomson Financial Securities Data

The contribution of M&A to shareholder value and economic efficiency is well known and does not differ in Europe from the USA.

First, if a company is performing below its potential, and its share price reflects this, an acquirer can benefit by buying this company at its present trading price (plus, in many cases, a control premium) and replacing its management with a new team capable of delivering this company's full potential. In this case, as long as the price paid for this company is lower than its maximum potential value, both sets of shareholders benefit. The acquirer's shareholders benefit from the additional value generated, while the selling shareholders benefit from being able to sell their stock at a higher price than they could have done in the open market. If the target company is bought for stock rather than cash, then its shareholders benefit from being able to participate in the increased value that will be generated in their stockholdings by the new management team.

Second, alternatively, even if a company is operating at its full stand-alone potential, the existence of synergies between this and another company offers the opportunity for value creation through a merger as the value of the combined entity will be greater than the sum of the two stand-alone values. As long as the control premium paid by the buyer is lower than the value of synergies sought and transaction expenses, the transaction will create value. This creation of value can be impressive, as shown in the case of the merger of Ciba-Geigy and Sandoz in Switzerland which gave birth to Aventis (Figure 6.4).

The outcome of mergers and acquisitions is not always as spectacular and their overall results are on the average quite disappointing.

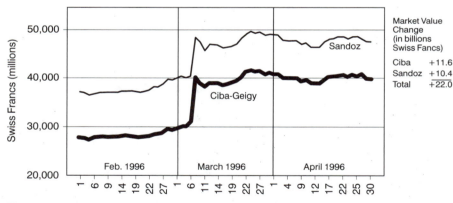

Figure 6.4 Market value, Ciba-Geigy and Sandoz

6.3.1 *Some doubtful results*

A number of studies have been conducted, on both European and North American transactions. The research tried to determine whether the enormous volumes of M&A activity witnessed since the early 1980s has actually delivered the promised value. The results of such studies are rarely conclusive, but the majority cast severe doubts over the value-creation of a great number of M&A deals.

Earlier this year, *The Economist* reported that a survey of studies of past merger waves found that, on average, two out of every three deals did not work, with the only winners being the shareholders of the acquired firm who got to sell their stock at an excessively high valuation.[13] Table 6.7 gives a non-exhaustive list of the seven 'deadly sins' of mergers and acquisitions.

Table 6.7   The seven deadly sins of M&A

1. Paying too much
2. Assuming a boom market won't crash
3. Leaping before looking
4. Straying too far afield
5. Swallowing something too big
6. Marrying disparate corporate cultures
7. Counting on key personnel staying

The European business environment has not been traditionally conducive to allowing M&A to be used for the creation of shareholder value. Issues such as competitive positioning and market shares have been more important. There are many reasons for this European specificity.

First, there is the traditional prevalence of stakeholder mentality over shareholders' best interests. Part of Europe's cultural history is entrenched in paternalistic notions of state and enterprise sharing the responsibility for the greater social good, and with this mindset, business acquisitions have not always been made with a view to immediate value creation.

Also, the lack of a historical equity culture in Europe, and the comparative underdevelopment of equity markets in Europe relative to the USA (see section 1 of this chapter) had smothered market forces. This lack of a large, institutional investor base, as exists in the USA, took a certain degree of pressure off European management teams. Furthermore, as was mentioned earlier, rigid labour laws and powerful trade unions have hindered any moves that would imply layoffs. In Germany, the labour representatives of any company have a seat on the board alongside management, and are therefore unlikely to agree to labour-cutting plans, irrespective of their potential to create incremental value.

[13] 'After the deal' *The Economist*, 9 January 1999

In addition, the market for corporate control has been extremely inefficient because of large cross-shareholdings that make it difficult to target a company if its other corporate owners disagree with the transaction. For example, the German insurance company Allianz has for years used its 21% interest in Dresdner Bank to block any merger talks with Deutsche Bank. Another source of inefficiency in the market for corporate control comes from the high degree of concentration in share ownership, which makes it difficult to target any company without the consent of the key shareholder. Colin Meyer of Oxford University found that in most continental countries the largest single investor controls over 30% of the shares, with as much as 50% in Germany and Italy. In the UK and USA, by contrast, these numbers are 10% and 5%, respectively, making the market for corporate control much more efficient.[14]

The problem of archaic unfriendly merger legislation should also be mentioned. For example, a French law, initially aimed at encouraging long-term investment in equities, allowed minority shareholders to double their voting powers if they have held their stock for more than two years. This was used in Promodes' bid for Casino, where the target company used this law for its defence.

The recent long fights in the French Banking Industry (BNP Societe Generale and Paribas) and in the French oil sector (Elf–Total–Petrofina) show how difficult are hostile takeovers in Europe. For these main reasons, most M&A activity had to be done on friendly, cooperative terms over the years, thus stifling the discipline that the hostile takeover 'threat' imposes on the management of a company.

6.3.2 New trends in the European landscape in M&A

The extraordinary value creation of the American economy over the last decade has raised interest all over the world. This had a significant influence on management philosophy in Europe and has been reflected in the European M&A market by the recent emergence of hostile transactions. A case in point was Krupp's initially hostile attack on its competitor Thyssen. The thoroughness with which the attack had been prepared (especially the pre-arrangement of the necessary financing) was so overwhelming that Thyssen, recognizing the inevitability of the deal, negotiated for a friendly merger. A banker close to the transaction later reported that the deal that was finally struck was better for both companies than Krupp's initial proposal. Other deals, like the Promodes–Casino transaction in France, went the other way, starting with a friendly approach and developing into a hostile one once the

---

[14] 'The price of friendliness: why Europe should learn to love takeover battles', *Mergers & Acquisitions Magazine*.

initial advance was rejected. Perhaps the most striking example of this, however, has been the battle for control of Telecom Italia.

Equally important as the new focus on shareholder value is the creation of a single European market through the introduction of the Euro. This has helped to level the playing field enormously among pan-European competitors, and to toughen the competitive marketplace for all. Potential acquirers for an under-performing company now can come from any corner of Europe, whereas previously they were more likely to be restricted to the domestic market. An example of this can be found in the European insurance industry. What is interesting about this example is not only the variety of nationalities of the parties involved, but also the fact that, once the initial bid had been made, another series of related mergers was initiated throughout Europe. For example, once BAT (which owned a number of insurance companies) bid for Zurich Insurance, Assicurazioni Generali of Italy bid for Assurances Generales de France (AGF) and Sweden's Nordbanken also announced plans for a merger. Although AGF was subsequently saved by a white-knight bid from Germany's Allianz, the catalyst of the initial bid helped launch a wider-spread European consolidation effort.

Another important change is the 'equitization' of European institutional investors and the fact that they are increasingly prepared to take action against the management teams of under-performing companies. In addition, the deregulation of the pension fund industry has increased both individual investors' awareness of stock performance and the power of the large institutional shareholders. This has been further emphasized by the creation of funds such as Hermes Lens Fund Management or UK Active Value, a fund aiming to invest in under-performing companies and then force the management to implement the appropriate actions to turn them around. An indicative example of such intervention is UK Active Value's investment in the Mirror Group (newspapers) and in Bullough (office furniture). The Swiss investor Martin Ebner is also practising American-style interventionist investing in Switzerland.

European governments are now increasingly accepting the possibility that foreign firms may buy the 'crown jewels' of their domestic economies. One sector where this can be seen is the automotive sector, where Fiat and Peugeot have teamed up to make mini-vans, as have VW and Ford. A more recent example is the Olivetti attack on Telecom Italia, where German partners are considered acceptable alternatives to the domestic attacker, provided certain criteria are met.

On a more 'technical' level, the dramatic recent drop in interest rates in Europe has now made it significantly cheaper than ever before for companies to borrow money with which to finance acquisitions. To this effect, the development of the high-yield debt market in Europe has added further fuel to the M&A fire. Further help has come from the innovative developments of the syndicated loan market, that has added flexibility to financing new deals. For instance, the loan for the ICI purchase of Unilever chemical business was structured in such a way that it was fully transferable without approval from the borrower. This transaction was highly unusual for the syndicated loan market, which is based on the borrower–lender relationship, but the extra flexibility granted by this feature made the deal easier to finance.[15] For those that do not like the idea of leverage, acquisitions can always be financed with equity, and the dramatic recovery of the European equity markets since August 1998 has given European corporations a strong acquisition currency.

6.3.3 A promising outlook

As European union takes place, companies that were formerly 'in play' domestically are now available to be bought by a much wider pool of potential companies. Furthermore, to benefit fully from the added efficiencies that such a wider potential M&A pool will bring, European governments will have to lift the presently restrictive labour laws and accept the labour implications of large cross-border M&A deals in order to help increase their overall domestic productivity.

A further trend to be expected is that Europe will see more deals done on the basis of 'merger of equals' than before. The benefit of such deals is that there is no control premium to pay, which increases the likelihood that both companies' shareholders will benefit from the transaction. Examples of such transactions are deals like BP/Amoco, Daimler/Chrysler, Credito Italiano/Unicredito. The drive for global reach is likely to continue to bring more cross-border transactions.

Obviously, all transactions driven by issues like strategic positioning or the achievement of international reach are ultimately driven by the longer-term goal of shareholder value, but its realization is contingent on a number of tricky implementation challenges. We believe that European companies will continue to consolidate for strategic reasons. Having done so, they will then focus on cost-cutting and other shareholder value creating initiatives as a second step.

6.4 Spin-offs, demergers and carve-outs in Europe

Against the background of the biggest ever wave in European M&A, it may seem a paradox to discuss break-up transactions such as

---

[15] 'Europe's takeover boom gathers pace', *Euromoney*, December 1997.

spin-offs and carve-outs as restructuring tools. However, these divestiture formats which make companies smaller and leaner are in fact closely connected with the current M&A boom. As discussed in the previous section, M&A activity in the 1990s was driven by the need to increase competitiveness on a pan-European or even global basis. We observed strategically motivated acquisitions in core areas and the dismantling of the unwieldy conglomerates pieced together over previous decades. Through corporate restructuring, European companies now grow and shrink at the same time, using spin-offs and carve-outs to focus their business on its core operations and to unlock hidden value by separating subsidiaries. In fact, spin-offs have already been heralded by many as the restructuring tool of the future, the means to prepare sprawling European companies for competition in the new millenium.[16]

We define a spin-off as a transaction in which a parent company transfers the business to be divested into a new subsidiary, and then distributes the shares of this subsidiary to its shareholders. After a spin-off, the new subsidiary is a separate publicly traded company, with a shareholder base identical to that of the parent company. In contrast, in a carve-out transaction, a parent divests a subsidiary by selling some or all of its shares in the subsidiary in a stock offering to the public, thereby raising cash from a new set of shareholders.

Carve-outs have traditionally been less popular than spin-offs due to the time involved in getting the offering registered, conducting road shows for investors, and ensuring that the business unit is a viable independent company. Carve-outs are also highly sensitive to equity market conditions. General advantages of carve-outs include the fact that they raise cash and help to broaden a company's investor base.

European spin-off and carve-out activity has grown tenfold since 1990 and reached a total volume of USD 34 billion in 1998. Before 1990 these transactions were virtually non-existent in most European countries. Figure 6.5 shows European spin-off and carve-out volumes in the 1990s.

Despite this increase, European firms preferred trade sales as divestiture format. According to the Securities Data Corporation, for the period from 1990 to 1998, sales to strategic or financial buyers accounted for 87% of European divestiture volume. Spin-offs accounted for 10% and carve-outs for only 3%.

During the 1990s, the UK alone accounted for approximately 50% of total stock break-up volume and 40% of all transactions. The geographic distribution was particularly unbalanced for spin-offs, with the UK and Sweden accounting for 80% of all transactions. Italy

[16] Anthony Currie, 'Spin-offs in a spin', *Euromoney*, January 1998

US$ bn

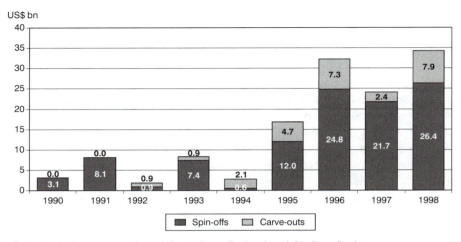

* Transaction size determined as market capitalization of spun-off entity at the end of the first trading day.
  Transactions included when either the parent company or the spin-off subsidiary were European.
Source: Securities Data Company, J.P. Morgan.

Figure 6.5   European spin-off and carve-out volume, 1990–1998

and the Netherlands recorded few spin-offs. To this date, no spin-offs have been recorded in Germany. Carve-outs occurred more evenly across Europe.

6.4.1 Specific barriers in the European context

The overall lag behind the USA, the preference for trade sales as a means of divestiture and the uneven geographic distribution of stock break-ups are the result of regulatory and systemic constraints in Europe that limited the attractiveness of these restructuring tools. Specific barriers include taxation, the underdeveloped capital markets as well as differences in corporate mentality and governance. As we will see later, important changes have been underway in Europe, which reduced some of these barriers and fuelled the flow of stock break-up transactions.

   Taxation is the most obvious and critical determinant of spin-off and carve-out activity, whereby transactions can be tax-efficient at the parent company and/or the shareholder level. For carve-outs, unlike in the USA, there are no tax advantages in Europe. Parent firms incur capital gains tax on issue proceeds in excess of the book value of the shares sold to the public. For spin-offs the situation is more favourable. Nevertheless, in only a few European countries is the tax system as conducive to spin-offs as it is in the USA. In principle, European Directives provide that tax-free spin-offs can be done as long as specific conditions are met. These conditions include that (a) the spun-off entity must carry on an active business; (b) the spin-off is not done with a view to preparing the spun-off entity for sale to a third party; (c) the spun-off entity needs to be tax-resident in the same country as the parent.

It is important to realize that taxation – like the other constraints – is idiosyncratic to particular countries. Germany and France in particular have adopted rather restrictive interpretations of these European guidelines, especially the conditions with respect to a subsequent change in ownership. For instance, German rules required 80% of the shareholders to hold their shares (and presumably register that holding) for a period of 5 years after the spin-off if the transaction is to be tax-free. Together with punitively high tax rates, this rule has effectively inhibited spin-offs in Germany. France, which has similarly restrictive rules and high taxes, has recorded only one spin-off transaction to date. As German and French conglomerates tried to restructure their portfolios, the prohibitive taxation of spin-offs forced them into long, complex and costly restructuring programmes. For example, it took Germany's Hoechst five years to rearrange its portfolio into a focused life sciences company, whereas its Swiss rival Sandoz carved out its speciality chemicals business Clariant and Novartis spun off Ciba SC in one single transaction.

The requirement to obtain a favourable ruling by the national tax authorities has been a further inhibitor of spin-off activity in Europe. Only in the UK is obtaining such a ruling a common process. In many other countries, it is more complicated and cumbersome. Overall, the tax rules explain the historically low level of stock break-ups in Europe and the uneven geographic distribution of transactions. Table 6.8 gives a general overview of the tax legislation in different European countries.

Investors have not been very receptive to smaller stock issues associated with spin-offs and carve-outs. The main reason was the lower liquidity of capital markets in continental Europe. The low trading volumes resulted in little research coverage for small stocks. This helps to explain why stock break-ups in Europe are heavily skewed towards large transactions. Between 1990 and 1998, there were 23 spin-offs and seven carve-outs in excess of US$1 billion. These transactions accounted for 80% of the total stock break-up volume. Carve-outs, which involve a public offering, faced additional barriers. Stock exchange listing requirements in most European countries were generally more restrictive than in the USA. Furthermore, transaction costs were high since, in many European countries, the equity issuance business lacked competition. In Germany, France and Switzerland, the equity issuance business was dominated by a handful of powerful universal banks. These banks

Table 6.8   Tax treatment of spin-offs in Europe

United Kingdom	Very common process. Spin-off requires tax ruling, but authorities are usually fairly flexible to allow commercial goals to be achieved. Example: Hanson/US Industries
Germany	Rules that allow tax-free spin-offs exist, but are unworkable in the context of widely held public companies. Tax rules have effectively precluded spin-offs to date
France	Rules are very complex and rely upon favourable ruling given by the tax authorities. Chargeurs/Pathé in 1996 was the only French spin-off to date
Italy	Tried and tested rules for achieving tax-free spin-offs exist. Examples: Gemina/HPI and Telecom Italia/TIM
Sweden	Historically restrictive rules have been relaxed. Spin-offs using 'Lex Asea' are relatively common. Example: Volvo/Swedish Match
Switzerland	Ciba Specialty Chemicals/Novartis was the first spin-off in Switzerland. Tax rules were written based on this transaction. The procedure is relatively complex and dependent on obtaining tax rulings. However, authorities can be helpful in overcoming these barriers
Netherlands	New rules with effect from 1 January 1998. Example: KPN/TNT and Vendex/Vedior
Finland	New rules introduced in September 1997 provided flexible regime to undertake spin-offs. As of yet no spin-offs have been recorded

Source: Adapted from Morgan Stanley internal documents

often had little interest in bringing a small carve-out issue to the market which needed their continued research support. They found it more profitable to trade high-volume blue-chip stocks.

Another barrier to stock break-ups was a cultural bias towards big corporations and a lack of entrepreneurship in countries such as Germany, France and Italy, which shaped the attitudes of divisional managers. These middle managers often lacked the ability and the willingness to run an independent company. In continental Europe, no equity-based financial incentives existed that could have motivated these managers to extradite themselves from the anonymous ranks of a big corporation and run their own business. Thus, even if a business was divested, a trade sale was preferred to the creation of an independent company because of the scarcity of qualified divisional management.

Additional barriers to stock break-ups were to be found in the approval and consent issues. In countries with strong worker representation, the human resources issues involved in spin-offs required the consent of labour. For instance, in a German parent corporation, the works council would have to approve the number of employees moving to the spun-off entity, any planned layoffs and any changes to the parent company's pension plan. Other potential compliance issues in some countries included regulatory and other third party consents for the spin-off, requirements of shareholder votes and requirements to register the newly issued securities.

6.4.2 The main drivers of break-up activity in the 1990s

First, European companies are increasingly using spin-offs and carve-outs to clarify their core business by divesting non-core activities and positioning them for future growth through mergers and acquisitions. As the deal flow in the pharmaceutical and chemical sectors suggests, spin-offs are a useful tool and often the quickest way to accomplish these strategic objectives, especially in fast consolidating industries. As in the USA, European companies have also dismantled the conglomerates they had assembled in previous years. The break-up of Hanson in the UK had probably similar symbolic power in Europe to that of ITT in the USA. A model of diversified business in the 1980s, Hanson spent most of the 1990s taking itself apart again.

Second, European companies also seek to unlock hidden value in a subsidiary by spinning it off altogether or carving out an equity stake because financial markets currently put a premium on 'pure plays'. As we shall see later, these transactions have not always created value, especially when the spun-off entity was already fully valued and the costs of separation exceeded the benefits of independence, or, in other cases, where the carved-out entity was not fully separated from the parent.

Contextual changes in Europe have certainly facilitated the increasing adoption of stock break-ups across Europe. Again, taxation is the most important factor. While rules for carve-outs have not notably changed, recent improvements in certain countries in the taxation of spin-offs were partly responsible for the record level of activity since 1996. When Sweden relaxed its restrictive rules, it triggered a whole wave of spin-offs with 11 of the total 13 transactions executed since 1996. The US$5 billion spin-off of Ciba SC from Novartis in 1997 was the first spin-off in Switzerland. Swiss tax rules were subsequently modelled on this precedent. While the rules are complex, they should enable more spin-offs in the future. Similarly, a favourable change in the local tax laws in 1998 has already produced two very large spin-offs in the Netherlands. Finland also introduced new rules in 1997.

Tax authorities in Germany and France, however, have resisted this movement throughout the period. They view a spin-off as a distribution of income or capital and tax it accordingly, whereas, in the rest of Europe, tax authorities appropriately regard structured spin-offs as a re-arrangement of investments the investor already owns. The process of European harmonization makes future changes conceivable. More importantly, it should dawn on the German and French governments that these tax rules amount to a serious competitive disadvantage for local companies in an era where restructuring is becoming increasingly the norm rather than the exception.

Another important driver has been the increasing availability of equity-based financial incentives. While still small in comparison with the USA, it must be assumed that, in Europe, share and stock option plans have increased the relative attraction of stock break-ups compared to trade sales. Independence gave spun-off businesses in Europe their own paper currency not only to pursue acquisitions, but also to motivate their managers. In the parent company, most of these managers did not have access to stock option plans. In this sense financial incentives helped the parent company, the spun-off entity and the managers involved to achieve their objectives by increasing the efficiency, performance and value of the spin-off and by spreading value-based compensation to a larger group of managers. As compensation of European executives continues to shift from company size to shareholder value creation, stock break-ups will continue to flourish in the future.

Capital markets in Europe have also become more liquid during that period, although Continental European markets still significantly lag behind the UK and the USA. Stock break-ups and liquid capital markets are interdependent. On the one hand, stock break-ups, in addition to other IPOs and privatizations, certainly helped the development of more liquid and efficient capital markets in Europe. On the other hand, stock break-ups also relied on liquid capital markets. In the future, the revolution in European pension systems is expected to provide unprecedented liquidity to European capital markets and will dramatically improve conditions in particular for smaller-sized equity issues.

There has been no evidence so far in Europe of fraudulent motivations for spin-offs. While creditors are the one constituency most adversely affected by spin-offs, e.g. through subsequent credit downgrades as in the case of Ciba SC, as of now, there is no recorded incident in which a company has damaged its creditors by transferring valuable assets to its shareholders. This is generally referred to as 'fraudulent conveyance' in the USA and happens when troubled firms spin-off a promising and profitable subsidiary to its shareholders.

6.4.3 *Value creation through break-ups*

The question remains whether European stock break-ups have created value for shareholders or whether they are just a new faddish divestiture technique that captured the imaginations of corporate leaders in Europe. Overall, evidence suggests that European spin-offs and carve-outs, on average, have created value. However, if not appropriately structured or ill-conceived, these transactions can produce severe disappointments for shareholders.

A study by J.P. Morgan[17] on European spin-offs since 1990 looked at excess returns, relative to the local stock market index, generated by the parent, the spun-off entity and the two combined. It showed that the announcement of the intention to execute a spin-off resulted in a 1.6% average excess return at the parent firm level, measured from ten days before announcement to seven days after announcement. This excess return increased to 3.4% by the date of execution. A more substantial re-rating occurred only over the months subsequent to the execution. Compared to the USA where announcements of spin-offs are usually very well received by the capital markets, these returns seem a rather modest response. Potential reasons include insufficient communication strategies outlining the benefits of the separation and recognition that the business was actually fully valued. Combined excess returns, the key measure of value creation, rose from an average 3.5%, from ten days before the announcement date to the execution date, to 14.0% at 12 months after separation and 12.0% at 24 months, before slipping to 7.1% at 36 months after separation. These results are summarized in Figure 6.6.

The study suggests that value-destroying transactions have been the result of poor operating performance at the parent or spin-off level subsequent to the separation. This emphasizes that, while a spin-off can highlight poor operating performance, it cannot improve it. For under-performing businesses a spin-off created value if it was part of a wider restructuring programme. However, where the parent was fully valued, spin-offs failed to live up to their expectations and in some cases even destroyed value. The most notable example is Hanson PLC in the UK, which had a market capitalization of US$20 billion before it broke up. After a series of four spin-offs, the combined market capitalization of the separate entities was only US$17.4 billion.

In a similar study, J.P. Morgan analysed the European carve-out market since 1990.[18] The study found that the announcement of a

[17] Paul Gibbs, 'Used properly, spin-offs simplify restructuring and create value, but they can't cure poor operating performance' J.P. Morgan Global Mergers & Acquisitions Review, 20 April 1999.

[18] Gibbs, Paul, 'European carve-outs create value, but only when the parent cedes control', J.P. Morgan Global Merger & Acquisitions Review, 1998.

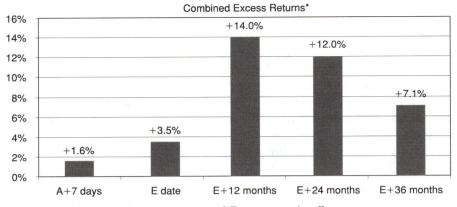

Figure 6.6 Combined excess returns of European spin-offs
Source: J. P. Morgan, *op.cit.*

carve-out triggered a modestly positive response. Average excess returns for the parent firm were just below 2%, measured from one week before the announcement to one week after the announcement. This number increased to 6% in the six months after the announcements. However, there was a wide dispersion of results between different transactions. The data suggests that in successful carve-outs, parent companies gave up control of their subsidiaries. These parent firms used carve-outs to clarify their business. The average excess return for parents that carved-out 100% of the subsidiary was 14% after six months. In contrast, where parents retain significant majority stakes in their subsidiary, the carve-out destroyed value for shareholders. The excess return for carve-outs where the parent retained more than 50% of the shares in the subsidiary was negative, at minus 1%. The study also found that larger carve-outs, relative to the parent, created more value, because the transaction had a more significant impact on its stock price.

   In summary, European carve-outs were more successful where the carve-out entity was large, relative to the parent, and where the parent ceded control and created a truly independent company. Similar to spin-offs, carve-outs were more successful as part of a wider restructuring programme that addressed operating performance. Independence of the subsidiary was a more important factor of value creation than unlocking hidden value in a subsidiary.

6.4.4 A potentially rich outlook

Given its overall positive track record, corporate restructuring in Europe will continue, and spin-offs and carve-outs will play an increasingly important role. The utilities sector is a good example. With currently over 2,500 utilities preparing themselves for the liberalization of the energy markets across Europe, there is a great expectation that this will lead to a significant amount of consolidation over the next few years. Many of the larger players have already announced cost-cutting programmes. The winners will spin-off non-core businesses to position themselves, and the spun-off entities will be ready for future growth through subsequent mergers and acquisitions.

Over the past few months, several big European companies have already made announcements or taken preparatory steps with respect to a potential spin-off of a subsidiary. For instance, Royal Dutch/Shell group announced plans to divest 40% of its chemical assets worth an estimated US$5 billion by spin-off or trade sale. In Germany, Hoechst has announced the spin-off of its industrial chemicals operations. This would mark the first spin-off in Germany. In what would be the biggest European spin-off to date, Deutsche Telekom is evaluating the spin-off of its cable business. In France, Vivendi announced the listing of a minority stake of its waste treatment, water and energy business.

In searching for further companies or industries that are likely to drive the flow of spin-offs over the next years, the following criteria can be applied:

- The parent company stock is under-performing. This is often the compelling reason for a stock break-up.
- Industries that do not have a pan-European presence. As these sectors consolidate, companies will continue to divest from peripheral activities. Spin-offs are often the quickest way to accomplish their objectives.
- Companies which should separate capital intensive, highly leveraged businesses from high growth businesses.
- The entity to be spun-off has not reached its full potential. Reasons could include, among others, strong internal competition for limited resources, such as management time, capital, . . .
- The entity to be spun-off can easily be separated from the group. There are few operating synergies, and allocation problems can be overcome.
- Other divestiture routes either are not available or unattractive (entity to be spun-off is too big or a trade sale would involve some anti-trust issues . . .).

6.5 Share repurchase in Europe[19]

Share repurchases have been widely used in the USA as a means to distribute cash to shareholders by mature companies running out of

[19] This section draws from 'Share-buybacks: the European and Japanese experience', by M. Bertoneche, Harvard Business School, note 9–298–134.

natural growth opportunities. This practice is increasingly adopted today by European firms as one way to enhance shareholder value, even if, with an average of 0.3% of market capitalization, it remains very modest compared with more than 3% annually in the USA.[20] From about $1 billion annually in the early 1990s, share buy-backs have reached some $22 billion in 1998. The UK, where legislation is the most favourable in Europe, maintains a dominant position, accounting for over 70% of European repurchases in recent years as shown in Figure 6.7, but share buy-back activity has increased significantly in some other European countries such as Sweden and France.

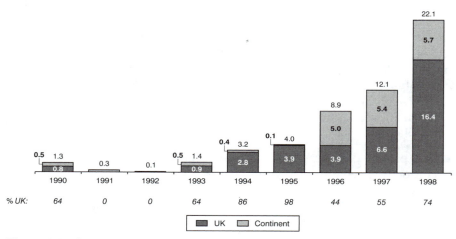

Figure 6.7   Share repurchase in Europe
Source: J.P. Morgan, '*Global Mergers and Acquisitions Review*', 1/27/99

6.5.1 Changing practices throughout Europe

What happened, in fact, for a long time and until recently in Europe is that companies have spent (and very often wasted) their big cash balances in unwise diversification policies, risky and expensive acquisitions, complicated cross-participations and unsound and ill-managed expansion strategies, anything but giving back the money to shareholders. European shareholders today, whether private or institutional, are changing, following the American example, and starting to refuse either the poor capital management and the sub-optimization of their resources in low-return cash balances or the frenetic and aggressive process of capital wasting including diversification, conglomeration and vertical integration, where size was more important than profitability. They consider themselves the best

---

[20] 'Share buy-backs: the fifth element', Morgan Stanley Dean Witter, 11 February 1998.

authority to decide upon the use of their own cash balances. Buy-backs are therefore an essential part of the process by which capital is recycled from mature companies with limited investment opportunities to young businesses with huge growth potential and enormous financing needs.

Share repurchases can also help progressively to sell off the mutual cross-holdings, designed to cement business relationships and create a system of core shareholders, particularly high in countries like France, Germany and Italy and significantly to reduce the stock ownership by the state and state-owned institutions. 'These mutual cross-participations and state ownership have proved to be more a handicap to stock performance than a support.'[21]

6.5.2 The driving forces behind this change

Perhaps the biggest catalyst behind the increase in share repurchase activity is the dramatic change in legislation that continues to take place throughout Europe. Both France and Germany recently passed laws which give companies the freedom to repurchase up to 10% of their share capital. In addition, tax laws in France were amended so as to reduce the tax on the proceeds from buy-backs to the lower capital gain rate rather than the previously higher marginal income tax rate. Finland legalized buy-backs in September 1997. The abolition of the Advanced Corporation Tax (ACT) in the UK simplified the process and provided more incentive for share repurchases.

These legislative changes represent a significant move in the development of a European culture, free from the interference of governments and an increasing recognition of the importance of shareholder value. A summary of the current legislation and tax regulation on share repurchase in various European countries is included in Table 6.9.

In addition to legal and fiscal changes, there are other drivers of future growth of the share repurchase programmes in Europe:

- Low interest rate environment
- Significant cash balances resulting from healthy free cash flow
- Overcapitalization of leading European companies' balance sheets
- Excess capacity in several segments of the industry
- Increased focus on EVA, the cost of equity and the weighted average cost of capital
- Pressure from US and other international investors

[21] CS First Boston, 'Shareholder value in Europe', 18 April 1996 p.6. See also CS First Boston, 'Share buybacks revisited', 11 February 1998.

Table 6.9 Survey of European share repurchase legislation and taxes

	Austria	Belgium	Denmark	Finland	France	Germany	Italy
Can you purchase your own shares	No (financials may repurchase up to 5%)	Yes	Yes	Yes	Yes (unless loss-making)	No	Yes
Shareholder approval required? Q=quorum M=Majority		Q: 50% M: 80%	M: Simple	Q: One shareholder M: 2/3	Q: 1/3 M: 2/3		Q: 50% M: Simple
Window period after shareholder vote		18 months	18 months		12 months		18 months
Maximum buy-back possible		10%	10%	5%	10%	10%	10%
Repurchased share can be cancelled or resold		Either	Either	Either	Either	Either	Either
Voting rights entitlement		Suspended	Suspended	Suspended	Suspended	Suspended	Suspended
Distributable reserve requirement		Yes	Yes	Yes	Yes	Yes	Yes
Tax treatment for shareholders: I=Individuals C=Comps. T=Tax exemp.		I: tax-free capital gain; C: taxable profits; T: exempt	I: taxable dividend income; C: taxable income; T: exempt	I & C: taxable capital gain; T: exempt	I: taxable gain; C: taxable dividend; T: dividend income	I: tax exempt gains, if held for period >6M; C: taxable income; T: no tax effect	I: taxable gain; C: taxable long-term investment taxed as gains; T: withholding tax
Any new legislation proposed or pending changes	No	No	No	Tax treatment has recently been subject to discussions; no further legislative actions taken yet	Expected only for clarification of uncertainties	Yes, major changes took place in 1998 via KonTraG law authorizing buy-backs	Ongoing reform of taxation of financial income.

	Netherlands	Norway	Portugal	Spain	Sweden	Switzerland	UK
Can you purchase your own shares	Yes	No	Yes	Yes	NO (Possible to redeem shares)	Yes	Yes
Shareholder approval required? Q=Quorum M=Majority	Q: 50% M: Simple		M: Simple	Q: 50% M: 66.75%	M: 2/3 with court approval	No. Only need approval to cancel repurchased shares	On Market: M: 75% + of those present at meeting
Window period after shareholder vote	None		18 months	18 months		None	18 months
Maximum buy-back possible	50%		10%	5%	(reduction to minimum capital, in by-laws)	10%	15% before going for a Tender Offer
Repurchased share can be cancelled or resold	Either		Either	Either	Cancelled	Either	Either (Recently changed)
Voting rights entitlement			No	Suspended	Suspended	Suspended	No
Distributable reserve requirement	Yes		Yes	Yes	Yes, for disbursement to shareholders	Yes	Yes *can be from proceeds of fresh issue
Tax treatment for shareholders: I=Individuals C=Comps. T=Tax exemp.	I: taxable dividend income; C: taxable gain at 35%; T: tax exempt		I: taxable gain; C: taxable gain; T: exempt	I: taxable gain; C: taxable gain	I&C: taxable capital gain; T: exempt Note: treated as dividend for witholding tax purposes	I: taxable income or tax-exempt gain; C: taxable income or capital gain; T: exempt	I&C: dividend income T: exempt
Any new legislation proposed or pending changes	No	New legislature affecting repurchases expected in 1999	No	Spanish Stock Exchange is to issue mailing setting out all requirements	Yes, new provisions in 1999 that will allow maximum 10% buy-back for public companies	As from 1998, own shares may be held for six years before partial liquidation is deemed	Tax credit to be reduced to 10% in April 1999 for individuals, but abolished for non-taxpayers/tax-exempts

Morgan Stanley Dean Witter research.
Salomon Smith Barney research.

Interest rates are likely to remain low for the near future in Europe. The low rates will continue to push companies towards buy-backs in two ways. First, the low return on cash balances, substantially lower than the weighted average cost of capital and the cost of equity capital will highlight the need, as shown in Chapter 4, to give money back to the shareholders. Second, the low pre-tax cost of borrowing will provide European executives with additional incentive to increase the level of leverage and use the proceeds of debt to repurchase shares. In addition to the low return on cash deposits, there is a significant 'agency cost'. The availability of significant cash reserves by European corporations represent a permanent temptation for management to make misconceived expenditures or pursue unprofitable projects or unwise acquisitions, as mentioned earlier.

The leverage levels appear to be low in most European industries with average ratios of net debt position/Enterprise value and EBIT/interest charges of 14% and five times respectively, as shown in Table 6.10.

Another survey of 391 public companies in Europe indicated that 105 (that is 27%) currently have a negative net debt position (or a positive net cash balance).[22] European executives need to find the appropriate level of leverage. The optimal capital structure should balance the tax benefits associated with increased debt and the higher risk of financial distress. Managers in Europe have, on average, been more risk averse, in recent years, than their US counterparts. European companies that have been reluctant to give up their high credit rating should probably reconsider the cost associated with such a financial policy.

The risk aversion to leverage could be partially explained by the grim prospects for in-court restructuring and harsh bankruptcy laws in most European countries described earlier. Furthermore, tax laws in some countries (UK, the Netherlands, Switzerland, etc.) had made it more attractive to maintain low debt levels and avoid share repurchases.

The growing maturity of several core European industries will reduce their level of capital expenditure in the near future. For example, in the automobile industry, techniques are adopted to minimize capital spending intensity by maximizing plant utilization and avoiding costly expansion. In the chemical sector, there is very little need for vast expenditure above maintenance, with several companies disposing of excess assets. Outsourcing strategies will also reduce the need for major capital expenditure. Over the next three years, 260 industrial companies in Europe are projected to generate over $200 billion of free cash flow in excess of their operating

[22] 'Share buybacks – the fifth element', Morgan Stanley Dean Witter, 11 February 1998.

Table 6.10   Leverage ratios and interest coverage in Europe

Industry	Net debt/ Enterprise value	EBIT/Total interest charges
Airlines	25%	4.3×
Auto	(25%)	3.4×
Building materials	52%	2.7×
Chemicals	21%	17.4×
Conglomerates	11%	5.6×
Construction	8%	1.8×
Food & Beverage	33%	2.3×
Food Retail	8%	7.0×
Healthcare	4%	21.9×
Hotel & Leisure	35%	2.1×
Industrials	50%	3.1×
Media	(7%)	52.6×
Metals & Minerals	23%	4.8×
Oil Field Services	18%	n.d.
Oils	16%	5.6×
Consumer non-cyclical	5%	5.6×
Paper & Forest Products	8%	4.1×
Pharmaceutical	5%	4.0×
Retail	7%	7.9×
Steel	11%	10.6×
Technology	9%	1.3×
Telecom	14%	6.5×
Textile & Home Furnishing	32%	2.6×
Tobacco	7%	17.7×
Utility	22%	4.4×
Average	14%	5.0×

Source: Credit Suisse First Boston, 'Share buybacks revisited', 9/29/98, p.20.

requirements.[23] Unlike the ill-fated diversification strategies pursued by most European companies in the 1980s, it may be expected that a significant portion of this free cash flow will be given back to shareholders through share repurchase programmes.

There seems to be a growing recognition in Europe of the cost of equity capital, which represents a major break with the past, when European executives understood well the cost of debt (an explicit and contractual cost) but not the cost of equity (an implicit and 'moral' cost). Until recently, many of the top European managers assumed that the cost of equity was the same as the dividend yield of the

[23] 'The virtuous circle', Salomon Smith Barney, 16 July 1998.

company, i.e. something around 2% or 3%, and a few even thought it was equal to zero![24] This dramatic change in looking at the cost of equity capital has made management of companies in Europe aware of the very high costs associated with traditional strategies of piling up excess cash and ready to explore efficient ways to return this cash to shareholders through buybacks.

6.5.3 An overall positive signal

There seems to be a positive immediate effect of share buybacks on stock prices. In contrast to the USA, where numerous companies continue to complete their well-established share repurchase programmes, share buyback announcements in Europe, a new phenomenon, represent a major financial policy change and are greeted with investor euphoria.

In its analysis of 67 share repurchase programmes executed in Europe between 1990 and 1997, J.P. Morgan's study[25] shows that the market reaction to buyback announcements was strongly positive. An average excess return peaked at 9.7% four months following the announcement and levelled off to 8.1% after six months. There were 41 outperforming companies averaging 19.3% positive excess return six months from announcement.

However, the same study found that highly levered companies announcing a share repurchase may be penalized if investors believe that cash should be kept for cyclical downturns.[26] J.P. Morgan also conducted a study in 1999 on all identifiable share repurchase programmes in Europe since 1990.[27] The study concluded that the most popular percentage to repurchase in Europe has been in the range of 8 to 10%, with a median of 8.4% of total shares outstanding.

Unlike cash dividends that put pressure on European managers to maintain, at least, the same level in the future (dividends, like most drugs, are habit forming and potentially addictive!), buy-backs impose much less pressure and give managers more flexibility since they are easier to initiate or end. As a matter of fact, share repurchases can be analysed as an option provided to management either to execute the buy-back or, if some better uses for the capital arise, to wait for a more appropriate time. The value of this option can

---

[24] 'Wising up to shareholder value' Euromoney, March 1998.
[25] 'European companies discover the power of share repurchases', J.P. Morgan, 21 January 1998.
[26] The outperforming industrial companies had a debt-equity ratio of only 4%, while the under-performing companies had a debt-equity ratio close to 40%.
[27] 'Global merger and acquisition review', J.P. Morgan, 27 January 1999.

be viewed as rising in tandem with increases in the expected variability of future operating cash flow and with the emergence of new investment opportunities'.[28] This explains why 'stock repurchases are likely to be a superior alternative to dividends for distributing excess capital to investors, especially for companies confronting a riskier business environment'.[29] Moreover, dividends are imposed on all shareholders, while share buy-backs give them the choice to decide whether they want a distribution or an increased share of equity, without having to deal with the reinvestment problem of funds. This flexibility offers a rather elegant way to 'eliminate' the most pessimistic, fragile shareholders, the ones who would have been the first to tender their shares in the case of a hostile take-over. In fact, the message conveyed to the investors by a share buy-back is clear: 'You leave me or you love me!'

Furthermore, continental Europe will benefit from the use of share buy-backs to repurchase government stakes and untangle numerous webs of cross-shareholdings, which reduce the public 'free float' and lead to conflicts of interest that negatively impact shareholder value. The relative lack of liquidity of most European equity markets currently makes it more difficult to complete successful share buy-backs. The danger is that the announcement of the intention to do a share buy-back could drive up the stock price above a level at which it makes economic sense to repurchase the shares. Nevertheless, the increased equity ownership by pension funds, the privatization of government positions and the growth in local retail investors should help increase the market liquidity, which will eventually make it easier to complete large repurchase programmes.

Another benefit of share repurchase programmes relates to the issuance of executive stock options. It is estimated that approximately 15% of all US buy-backs are intended to offset employee stock option programmes.[30] While the number of European stock options is still lagging, one can expect a significant increase in performance incentive systems in the near future. Since dividends reduce the value of stock options under the Black and Scholes model, executives have an incentive to decrease dividends and return cash to shareholders through share repurchase programmes. In fact, the increase in stock options, along with the growth of high technology companies and a buoyant stock market, led to the

[28] Sotter, D., E. Brigham and P. Evanson, 'The dividend cut heard round the world: the case of FPL', *Journal of Applied Corporate Finance*, Vol. 9, Number 1, Spring 1996, p. 14.

[29] Ibid., p. 15.

[30] 'European share buybacks: full speed ahead', Morgan Stanley Dean Witter, 7 April 1998, p.7.

decrease of the US dividend yield from 3.5% to 1.5% in the 1990s. A study by Christine Jolls found firms which rely heavily on stock option compensation plans are significantly more likely to repurchase their shares than firms which rely less heavily on stock options to compensate top executives.[31]

6.5.4 A very promising outlook

As legal, fiscal and other barriers are gradually phased out, one can predict that the level of share repurchase activity in continental Europe will dramatically increase approaching US and UK levels in the near future. The following criteria can be used to identify attractive candidates for repurchase programmes in Europe:

- Strong financial condition and low debt/equity ratio and/or a significant excess cash balance.
- High cash flow coverage of both interest expenses and future investments in capital expenditure and additional working capital.
- Industry over-capacity problems or pressures on operating margins. This necessitates a reduction in invested capital through sale of assets or other forms of restructuring to support higher returns on invested capital.
- Management difficulties in finding attractive investment opportunities for utilizing excess cash balances, with decreasing returns on incremental capital.

When it comes to shareholder value, European countries (with probably the exception of the UK) have a long way to go. But things are changing and the globalization of capital markets has put increasing pressure on corporate management in Europe to focus on shareholder value. The spreading practice of share buy-backs is an illustration of such a change. Buy-backs are a vital part of the recycling process of capital flows from slow growth mature companies to young firms with high growth potentials. Most countries in Europe have many of the former category and too few of the latter. The capital markets should not be blamed for that. The causes are much deeper and relate to strong cultural features such as 'the excessive punishment for failure in business, narrow-minded views about the benefits of stock-options and other forms of equity participation for managers and the lack of importance attached to corporate governance.'[32]

[31] Jolls, C., 'Stock repurchase and incentive compensation', NBER Working Paper No. 6467, March 1998.
[32] 'Brussels to spur risk capital growth', *Financial Times*, 30 March 1998.

6.6 Shareholder value in Europe: some concluding comments

The arrival of the Euro and the political move towards deregulation in Europe have created an environment of great transparency where firms are more open to scrutiny by an ever wider audience. In addition, European firms are now competing on an increasingly global playing field, where they regularly find themselves head-to-head with their American rivals.

There is little doubt that the concept of shareholder value is now firmly in place in Europe. In part, this is due to the 'equitization' of European investors, coupled with the deregulation of the pension fund markets in most European countries and the emergence of American-style interventionist funds. In part, this shareholder focus in Europe may be explained by the international diversification of portfolios in European assets. Moreover, European companies are increasingly pursuing dual European–US stock listings in order to increase the liquidity of their shares, tapping a wider investor base. They have to submit themselves to the same level of disclosure and scrutiny than the US firms.

This is not, however, a story of the US model simply transferred and applied in Europe move for move. The cultural background and the social environment in Europe require that executives pay attention to the broader implications of their decisions and actions, particularly when they involve layoffs. In explaining his move to break up the proposed merger between Paribas and Societe Generale, the chairman of Banque Nationale de Paris said that, if its bank would acquire them both, the deal would 'enhance job security and stability'[33], not really the sort of statement that attracts value-driven shareholders.

If the increased adoption of value measurement, such as EVA, as performance assessment tool is the first step towards determining accurately the value created by managers, this still does not address the issue of compensation, where the high pay packages commanded by American managers would be considered, in most European countries, to be disrespectful towards the much more lowly paid workers. This is a particularly thorny issue in the cultural integration between Daimler and Chrysler, as many American managers may find themselves reporting to German executives with lower pay packages. From a cultural point of view, large pay inequalities do not sit well with more egalitarian minded Europeans. Daimler's passenger car development director, Jurgen Hubbert

[33] 'Hostile environs', *The Economist*, 13 March 1999.

'shudders to think of his reputation in his small town if it was reported that his pay had tripled'.[34]

There is little doubt, however, that these cultural issues will have to be addressed and dealt with in order to accommodate shareholder value focus. Maybe Europe won't shift all the way to the US end of the spectrum, especially as the USA now seems to be considering the virtues of managers focusing on a slightly wider 'radar screen'. But it will certainly be much more shareholder value oriented in five years' time than it is today.

The only potential threat in the development of shareholder value in Europe will come in the event of problems in the USA, such as a stock market crash or signs of severe civil unrest caused by the USA's extreme income inequality, beginning to cast a shadow of doubt over the validity of the US model. Even in that case, however, the concept of shareholder value is unlikely, in our opinion, to be abandoned completely. At most, it will be 'Europeanized' much more in its application.

Successful implementation of value-based management pro- grammes depends on being embraced wholeheartedly at the top of the organization. This way, it can trickle through the ranks and be applied successfully. This is probably why a number of success stories in Europe have been preceded by a change in the company's chief executive officer. The arrival of a new generation of young executives, sometimes trained in the USA, will certainly contribute to a more widespread adoption of shareholder-driven restructuring pro- grammes. Incentive enhancing pay-for-performance packages, using options and various other ways to align managers' interests with those of shareholders will also help in the successful implementation of these programmes. But there should also be no doubt that, as part of these changes, layoffs will occur. This happened in the USA, where the 500 largest firms shed 3.5 million jobs from 1973 to 1993. The answer to this difficult social issue comes not in stubbornly refusing to accept the world's economic realities but in managing to re-deploy success- fully this portion of the labour force in new value creating activities. This is what the USA has done where the 3.5 million jobs lost in the restructuring programmes have been more than offset by 16 million new jobs created during the same period through entrepreneurial ventures.

Europe will have to pursue the same strategy, and governments will have a crucial role to play in designing an environment where entrepreneurialism is encouraged, promoted and rewarded. Hope- fully, things are moving quite fast in Europe and governments are

[34] 'After the deal', *The Economist*, 9 January 1999.

taking active steps to establish a more creative risk-taking environment. This includes numerous radical changes both in personal as well as business legislation and this is also evidenced by the recent spate of growth in the number of venture capital funds opening in Europe or moving from the USA, aware of the changes taking place and aiming at capitalizing on them.

The concept of shareholder value has finally arrived in Europe and it is there to stay. This is not a temporary flirtation with a philosophy that seems to have worked in America. It is a very serious attempt by European managers to fill the competitive gap with their American rivals. The key driver for their success will be the passion with which they embrace the concept, blend it and distil it in a way appropriate for the European context, and the diligence with which they apply it as a comprehensive system for goal setting, performance measurement and professionals' compensation. The arrival of the Euro, despite its difficulties, has created an environment where not only can the restructuring process take place successfully but also where the resources that will be released through it can be more efficiently and profitably re-deployed. The net effect should be an even greater increase in welfare throughout the region.

Index

Accounting equation, 10, 11
Accounting policies:
    choice, 41
    European differences table, 168,
        169, 170
Accrual basis of accounting, 48–9,
    61
Accrued expenses, 35
Accrued liabilities, 35
Accumulated other comprehensive
    income, 31–3
Activity financing, cash used, 65
Additional paid-in capital, 30
Adjusted present value (APV)
    method, 124, 147, 150–3
    compressed, see Capital cash flow
        (CCF) method
Administrative costs, 50
Advanced Corporation Tax (ACT),
    abolition in UK, 191
Agency costs, barriers to change,
    170–1
American Motors Corporation
    (AMC), acquisition, 12, 13
Anglo-American practice:
    balance sheet style, 38, 40
    financial reporting style, 4, 22
    registered shares, 30
Asset Beta, see Beta, unlevered
Assets, 10, 11–12
    book value, 16
    increasing efficiency, 97
    market value, 16
    turnover, 80–1
    valuation, 137–9
    value formula, 137
Average tax rate, 120

Bad debt allowance, 22
Balance sheet:
    annotated, 4, 8
    DaimlerChrysler layout, 37–41
    historic, 16–17
    make-up, 10
    value-based, 17
Bankruptcy laws, barriers to
    change, 172–3
Bearer shares (German), 30
Beta, levered/unlevered, 117–18
Beta coefficient, 110–11, 114, 121
    table for some French companies,
        113
    table for some German
        companies, 114
    table for some UK companies, 112
Blended cost of capital, 119
Book valuation, 16
Business objectives:
    consistency test, 100
    effects of variable, 98–9
    targets, 98

Capital Asset Pricing Model (CAPM),
    121
    measuring expected returns,
        113–15
Capital cash flow (CCF) method,
    153–4
Capital stock, 29–30
    issuance proceeds, 66
    see also Shares
Carve-outs, 181–2, 188
Cash, 22
Cash balance, changes, 67–8

Cash cycle days, 88–9, 90–1
Cash equivalents, 22
Cash flow:
  expected, 142–3
  models, 98–100
Cash flow after tax (Cfloat), 69–70,
    78
Cash flow cycle, 89
Cash flow return on assets (RonA),
    78–9
Cash flow statement, 7, 57–60
  analysis, 72–3
  rearranged, 68–73
Comparables approach:
  acquisition analysis, 160
  company, 157, 158
  transactions, 157
Components approach (cash flow
    calculations), 142–4
Compressed APV, *see* Capital cash
    flow (CCF) method
Consolidated balance sheet, 4–5, 9
Contingent liabilities, 45
Convertible debt, 36
Corporate control, European
    culture, 178
Corporate restructuring, in Europe,
    188–9
Cost of assets, 117, 119
Cost of capital, 116–19
  blended, 119
  international economy, 128–9
  single/multiple, 124–8
  value creation measurement,
    129–32
Cost of debt, 116
Cost of equity, 117, 119
  European understanding, 195–6
Cost of sales, 48
Creditor days, 87–8
Current assets, 19–22
Current liabilities, UK/US different
    display practices, 40
Current ratio, 42–3, 86

DaimlerChrysler, background to
    selection, 3–4

Days sales in receivables (DSR),
    81–2
Debt equity ratio, 44, 84
Debt ratio, 11, 44, 84
Deferred income, 28, 37
Deferred tax, 23–7
  adjustments, 24–7
  assets, 26–7
  liabilities, 26–7, 37
  as non-cash item, 61
Depletion, 18
Depreciation, 17
  as non-cash item, 61
Derivatives, accounting records, 45
Direct costs, 49
Discount rates, risk-adjusted, 128
Discounted cash flow (DCF), 137–9
  APV method, 147, 150–3
  CCF method, 153–4
  ECF method, 154–6
  and economic value added, 161
  FCF-WACC method, 146–7
  table of comparison of methods,
    158
  valuation parameters, 141–6
Discounting, principle, 138
Dividend policy, 97
  effects, 93–4
  payment, 66–7
Dividend yield ratio, 102
duPont chart, financial health
    illustration, 91

Earnings Before Interest, Tax,
    Depreciation and Amortization
    (EBITDA), 69
Earnings Before Interest After Tax
    (EBIAT), 51, 69, 78, 130
Earnings Before Interest and Tax
    (EBIT), 51, 130
Earnings per share (eps), 54–5
  diluted, 55
Economic value added (EVA), 129,
    161
  definitions, 130–2
  European markets, 168
Effective tax rate, 52–3

Efficiency ratios, 80–3
  key purposes, 83
Employee pension fund, prepaid
  expenses, 27
Employee power, barriers to change,
  171–2
Employee shareholding, European
  markets, 167
Equipment on operating leases,
  18–19
Equity Beta, *see* Beta, levered
Equity cash flow (ECF) method, 154–6
Equity market risk premium, 114,
  115
  for European countries, 116
Equity market value, 118
Equity markets, European tradition,
  165
Euro:
  1999 introduction, 9–10
  creation of single European
    market, 179
  currency translation effects, 32
European culture:
  corporate restructuring, 188–9
  equity market recovery, 180
  mergers and acquisitions, 173–80
  share repurchase, 189–91,
    192–3, 196–8
  shareholder value, 199–201
  shareholder value change
    barriers, 168–73
  shareholder value change drivers,
    165–8
European Economic Community,
  common standards, 168
Exchange rates, effect on cash
  statements, 68
Executives:
  incentive schemes, 170–1
  remuneration, 199–200
Extraordinary items (on income
  statement), 54

FCF-WACC (free cash flow-weighted
  average cost of capital) method,
  146–7, 148–9

FIFO (first in first out) costing
  method, 20
Financial Accounting Standard
  Board, US, 45
Financial income, 51–2
Financial liabilities, 36
  repayments, 66
Financial market conditions,
  targets, 98
Financial policies:
  consistency test, 100
  effect of variable, 98–9
  targets, 98
Financial ratios, 74, 83–5
  key purposes, 86
  summary table, 102–3
Financial receivables, net changes,
  64
Financial services receivables, 21
Financing cash flows, 65–8
Fixed assets, 12–19
  net purchases, 63–4
Forecast period, 141
Fraudulent conveyance, 186
Free cash flow (FCF), 71–2, 142–4,
  161
Funding gap, 95
  alternative policies, 97
  origins, 96

Germany:
  Commercial Code, 31
  corporate law, 31
  corporate tax rate, 23, 52–3
  ownership registration, 30
Globalization:
  effect on cost of capital, 128–9
  US share ownership, 168
Goodwill, 12–16
  amortization as non-cash item, 61
Gross margin, 49, 50, 77
  ratio, 56
Group financials, 9
Growth relationships, 97–100

Historic cost convention, 28

Incentive schemes, executive, 170–1
Incidental income, 51
Income before extraordinary items, 53
Income statement, 6, 46–7
  alternative arrangement, 55–6
  equation, 48
  ratios, 56–7
Income taxes:
  total, 52
  see also Taxation
Information disclosure requirements, 168
Intangible assets, 12–17
Inter-company transactions, 9
Interest charges, European, 195
Interest coverage, 85
Interest coverage ratio, 57
Interest tax shield, 146, 147
Internal rate of return (IRR), 140–1
Interventionist investment, in Europe, 179
Inventories, 19
  changes, 62–3
Inventory days, 82–3
Investment, 18, 70
  cash flows, 63–5
  cash used, 63
  decisions, 139–41
  interventionist, 179

Labour market, barriers to change, 171–2
Leverage, 44–5, 117–18, 121–2
  European levels, 194
  increasing, 97
Leverage ratios, 84–5
  European, 195
Leveraged buyouts (LBOs), 123
Liabilities, 10, 29, 33–4, 35
LIFO (last in first out) costing method, 20
Limited liability concept, 29
Liquidation terminal value, 144
Liquidity ratios, 86–91
  key purposes, 89
Long-term financial assets, 18

Long-term growth, constraints, 93–7
Long-term liabilities, changes, 66
Loss on early extinguishment of debt, 52

Marginal tax rate, 120
Market imperatives, targets, 98
Market valuation, 16
Matching principle, costs and revenues, 24, 28
Merger costs, 51
Mergers and acquisitions (M&A):
  errors to be avoided, 177
  European culture, 173–8
  new European trends, 178–80
Minority interests (on income statement), 34, 52, 53

Net asset value, 29
Net current assets, 86
Net fixed assets (NFA), 133
Net income, 54
Net operating losses (NOLs), 23–4
Net present value (NPV), 139–41, 161
Net profit ratio, 54, 56
Net working capital (NWC), 43, 44, 70
Non-cash items, 60–1
NOPAT (net operating profit after taxes), *see* EBIAT

Off-balance sheet items, 45
Operating activities:
  cash provided, 60, 63
  costs, 50
Operational cash flows, 60–3

Paper borrowings, changes, 66
Par value (shares), 30
Payable days, *see* Creditor days
Payout ratio (PO), 93, 94
Pension funds, European markets, 167

Perpetuity approach, cash flow, 145
Preference shares/stock, 33
Premium on acquisition, 13
Prepaid expenses, 27–8
Price earnings ratio (per), 100–1
Price to book (P/B) ratio, 101
Privatization, European markets, 166
Product costs, *see* Cost of sales
Profit and loss approach (cash flow
    calculations), 142–4
Profit margin, 75, 77
Profitability ratios, 75–9
  key purposes, 80
Property, plant and equipment, 17
Prudence concept, 38

Quick assets, 43
Quick ratio, 43, 87

Receivables, 20–1
Registered shares, 30
Research and development costs, 50
Reserve accounting, 14
Retained earnings, 30–1
Retention ratio (RR), 94
Return on assets (ROA), 77–8
  relationship to ROE, 104–5
Return on capital employed (ROCE),
    129, 130, 133
Return on equity (ROE), 79–80,
    92–3
  key drivers, 91
  relationship to ROA, 104–5
Return on investment (ROI), 78, 81,
    93
Revenues, 48–9
Rhenish style of financial reporting,
    4, 22
Risk:
  assessing, 110–11
  types, 109, 111

Salvage value, 144
Securities, 22
Selling costs, 50

Share premium, 30
Share repurchase, 133, 136
  European practice, 189–91,
    192–3, 196–8
  increased activity, 191–6
  legislation and taxes, 192–3
Shareholder value, 133–6
  European change barriers,
    168–73
  European change drivers, 165–8
  European perspective, 164–5,
    199–201
Short-term growth, constraints,
    90–1
Short-term liabilities, changes, 66
Special distribution tax refund, 67
Spin-offs, 181–2
  selection criteria, 189
  tax treatment, 184
Statements of income, *see* Income
    statement
Stock break-ups:
  European barriers, 182–5
  progress, 185–6
  value creation, 187–9
Stock market performance
    measures, 100–2
Stock markets, European
    expansion, 166–8
Stock options, European markets,
    167
Stockholders' equity, 10, 29–33
Sustainable growth, drivers, 93–5
Sustainable growth rate (SGR), 94
Syndicated loan market, European
    developments, 180

Takeovers, hostile, 178
Tax credit carry forwards (US term),
    23
Tax environment, barriers to
    change, 173
Tax rate:
  average, 120
  effective, *see* Effective tax rate
  marginal, 120

Taxation, European constraints,
    182–3, 184
Terminal value, calculation, 144–6
Time horizon, 141
Timing differences, effect, 25
Trade liabilities, 36
Trade receivables, 20–1
Trade sales, European
    developments, 181, 182
Translation adjustments, currency,
    32
Treasury Stock, 33
    purchase, 66

US share ownership,
    internationalization, 168

Valuation:
    assets, *see* Asset valuation
    discounted cash flow approach,
        141, 146, 158
Value creation, 129–32, 162
    from stock break-ups, 187–9
Value drivers, 162, 163

Weighted average cost of capital
    (WACC), 119–22
    components, 123
    cost of assets relationship
        calculation, 124, 125–6
    free cash flow method, 146–7
    using, 123
Working capital, changes, 61–2